STYLE
AND
SUBSTANCE

Copyright © 2009 Filipacchi Publishing, a division of Hachette Filipacchi Media U.S., Inc.

First published in the United States of America by Filipacchi Publishing
1633 Broadway, New York, NY 10019

Edited by Margaret Russell
Art direction by Florentino Pamintuan
Editorial production by Dara Keithley
Art production and design by Katherine McDonald

ISBN: 978-1-933231-60-0

Library of Congress Control Number: 2009923651

Printed in China

STYLE
AND
SUBSTANCE

The Best of
ELLE DECOR

BY MARGARET RUSSELL

AND THE EDITORS OF
ELLE DECOR

CONTENTS

FOREWORD

It was 20 years ago that a small team of writers, editors, and art directors—a quirky mélange of experts and novices, both American and French—banded together to create a new magazine called ELLE DECOR. It was conceived as a sister publication to the U.S. edition of ELLE (then just a few years old) and propelled by the 1987 launch of French ELLE DÉCORATION, and our fashion heritage, international perspective, and keen focus on the synergy between interior design and the runway were considered groundbreaking at the time. I was perhaps the third person hired, and over the next six months did everything from filing to producing shoots to proofreading text before the first layouts shipped to press in late summer. Two decades later it's funny that so much—yet so little—has changed. Clearly, my role is different now, but our editorial mission remains every bit as relevant today as it was in 1989: ELLE DECOR celebrates where style lives.

The magazine's interiors share a distinct point of view, but we are open-minded in our outlook, embracing sensibilities that range from classic to cutting-edge. Our most beloved design characteristics? Personality, passion, joie de vivre, and flair. It's true, our most dazzling stories feature people with fearless style who don't care what others think—and those who are curious, confident, and cosmopolitan will always find a place in our pages. We believe that luxury needn't be expensive, great design can be had at little cost, and there's no reason affordable furnishings shouldn't be chic. And when offered a choice, we'll take a bit of patina and wear and tear over brand-spanking-new decor every time. Because worldly rooms never fail to seduce us; they show who you are, where you've traveled, and what you love—the perfect formula for ELLE DECOR.

We've scoured our archives to zero in on the most compelling interiors, our most intriguing and iconic images, and the most inspiring ideas, starting with our very first issue. These photos, along with insights and design tips from some of our favorite experts and stylesetters—from Albert Hadley to Valentino—salute the legacy of all who have contributed to ELLE DECOR. We hope that *Style and Substance* will be your room-by-room guide to living well.

MARGARET RUSSELL
VP/Editor in Chief, ELLE DECOR

INVITING INTERIORS

LIVING ROOMS

LIBRARIES & HOME OFFICES

DINING ROOMS

KITCHENS

LIVING ROOMS

Stunningly elegant, warmly traditional, or coolly minimal, all living rooms have a major element in common—comfort. They are, obviously, rooms for living, for relaxing at the end of the day by reading, watching television, or enjoying a conversation with family and friends. So when it comes to furnishing this important space, focus on reality rather than fantasy. "Your living room should grow out of the needs of your daily life," pioneering interior decorator Elsie de Wolfe wrote in her 1913 book *The House in Good Taste*. That advice from one of the design industry's early doyennes holds true nearly a century later. If smart parties, memorable hors d'oeuvres, and the perfect little black dress are defining aspects of your world, then a living room outfitted with refined, luxurious antiques and sumptuous silk damasks could be the ideal setting. For homeowners whose lifestyles are easygoing and enlivened by children or pets, casual materials designed to age well and hold up to daily wear and tear might be more appropriate, among them crisp linen and cotton, durable wool-mohair, tough but sophisticated leather, even sturdy denim or corduroy. Whether the desired atmosphere is practical or posh, though, certain commonsense rules apply. To contribute energy and interest, contrast scale and use a variety of silhouettes: Mix an oversize sofa and a stately bookcase with petite antique chairs in a room with soaring ceilings, or place one or two gutsy pieces in a cozy, compact space. Chairs and sofas should range from leanly tailored to invitingly plump, and a combination of furnishings with wood, metal, and painted surfaces adds visual and tactile excitement. Remember, lighting is as much about task as it is about illumination, from casting the right amount of light to read a book by to showcasing a work of art or a photo collection. Seek out occasional tables with character and place them within easy reach to offer guests somewhere to set a cup of coffee or a cocktail. And personal treasures are always the essential finishing touch. ■

PRECEDING PAGES
An English Regency recamier and a sculpture by
André Dubreuil add a note of civilized
informality to the living room of architect Lee F. Mindel's
Southampton, New York, cottage.

OPPOSITE
Decorator Albert Hadley used a framed
panel painted pale blue to set off a Jean-Michel Frank stool
and a minimalist console of his
own design at his prewar Manhattan apartment.

ABOVE
The living room of the West Village townhouse designer
Steven Gambrel shares with Chris Connor
features luxuriously deep tufted upholstery, curtains inspired
by a vintage naval uniform, and
a hand-loomed rug
patterned after a cable-knit sweater.

OPPOSITE
Architect Alan Wanzenberg created
a sense of rustic elegance at his
oceanfront retreat in Water Island, New York,
with vintage woven-raffia armchairs
by Charlotte Perriand and Dominique wood
chairs with canvas cushions;
the walls and ceiling are
sheathed in whitewashed cedar.

ABOVE
On Île de Ré, off France's
Atlantic coast,
Katherine Margaritis punctuated
the painted furniture, loosely slipcovered
seating, and tawny heart-of-pine
flooring of her ethereal
white-paneled sitting room with
one petite framed canvas.

LEFT
The card room at the Sag Harbor, New York,
house of Chris Connor and decorator Steven Gambrel
was painted shell-pink with a mix
of casein and natural pigments; a framed collection
of birds' eggs is displayed
over the settee, and the floorboards are
reclaimed 19th-century pine
from Maine.

OPPOSITE
Lemon-yellow curtains add drama to the living room of a 1950s Miami
house owned by financier Nicolas Berggruen, which was decorated by Stephen Sills
and James Huniford of Stephen Sills Associates. Tailored
Jules-Émile Leleu armchairs from the '40s are piped in white, the tables
are by René Prou, and the bench is Austrian.

ABOVE
In the living room of the main house at
Ricky and Ralph Lauren's Montauk, New York, compound, a banquette covered in
a Ralph Lauren Home linen stretches nearly the width
of the room. Cypress armchairs are pulled up to a cocktail table
by Wyeth and a Mies van der Rohe Barcelona daybed by Knoll, and the nickel
pharmacy lamps are by Ralph Lauren Home; the sunlight reflecting
on the ceiling—paneled in polished
gum plywood—creates a soft golden glow.

OPPOSITE
Designer David Collins discovered his
London living room's sapphire
velvet sofa and chairs, attributed to Jansen, at a flea market.
The stone-top bronze dining table is a 1920s
Raymond Subes piece; it is flanked by
a pair of vintage sycamore cabinets by Dominique.

ABOVE
Slate-blue linen curtains frame
a line of windows in the Chicago living room
of decorator Nate Berkus; the suzani throw was found in Istanbul,
and the woven-base tables are Mexican.
Joshua Tree, a photo work by Fernando Bengoechea,
and *America*, an oil-on-burlap work
by Remigio Gudin, are displayed on the far wall;
the leather-and-corduroy daybed
is 1940s French, and the rug was custom
made by Madeline Weinrib.

LEFT
The mirror above David Collins's living
room mantel is similar to one he designed for Harvey's,
one of his London restaurant projects;
it is based on a Giacometti original.

OPPOSITE
Decorator Muriel Brandolini designed
fanciful patchwork curtains of Florentine fabrics to
accentuate the double-height Upper East
Side living room of Moyra Mulholland and her husband.

TOP RIGHT
The Tribeca loft of artist Nabil Nahas is
laden with eclectic treasures;
his starfish painting *Red Venus* has pride of
place above a suite of Empire furniture.

CENTER RIGHT
Michelle Smith, designer of the fashion label
Milly, makes a signature statement in
the Manhattan apartment she shares with her family.
Decorator Shaun Jackson upholstered a pair
of vintage chairs in a Jim Thompson
zebra-stripe silk; the églomisé mirror is from the 1940s.

BOTTOM RIGHT
On Paris's Right Bank, antiques dealer Yves
Gastou and his wife, Françoise, assembled
an elegant mélange of midcentury furnishings
in their apartment, including a
wrought-iron grille by Gilbert Poillerat and
1937 André Arbus armchairs.

BELOW
For clients Carole and Richard Rifkind,
architects Shelton, Mindel & Associates
transformed a 1970s New York City apartment
into a streamlined setting for taxicab-yellow
Arne Jacobsen Egg chairs
and a Poul Kjaerholm cocktail table.

OPPOSITE
The walls, curtains, and
upholstery in stylesetter Lee Radziwill's
Paris apartment feature a
Le Manach chinoiserie fabric; a Peter
Beard photograph
is displayed on the wall.

ABOVE
Textile guru Lisa Fine
sheathed the walls and ceiling of her
Left Bank parlor in a sprightly
hand-blocked fabric and lacquered the
bookcases and cabinetry
lipstick-red; the
mirror is English Regency.

LEFT
The Manhattan living
room of designers Ward Denton
and Christopher Gardner is
painted a regal red; the bold color
glows in the evening
when illuminated by lamps
and candles.

ABOVE
Designer Jeffrey Bilhuber transformed
the Pennsylvania barn of Joanne
and Richard Stevens into a loftlike space that
functions as an afternoon sanctuary
and a nighttime party pavilion. Sleek red-lacquer
tables and seats, boxy furniture
cushioned with futons, and antique Windsor
armchairs are scattered around the
structure, which was taken down to its shell.

RIGHT
In a 1961 Richard Neutra
house perched high above Beverly Hills,
photographer Matthew Rolston and decorator
Ted Russell salute 20th-century
design with editions of Gerrit Rietveld's red
Utrecht armchair, Kubus
armchairs by Josef Hoffman, and a Projecteur
floor lamp by Mariano Fortuny.

OPPOSITE
Critic and art historian Georges
Bernier and his wife, Monique, enlivened a
space at their historic home
near Blois, France, with an energetic
Sonia Delaunay textile reproduced
by the Paris gallery Artcurial.

"IT'S ALL ABOUT EDITING
ONE'S LIFE—REFINING, SIMPLIFYING, CONSTANTLY
EDITING"

— *Bill Blass, fashion designer*

LEFT
An 1840s Long Island cottage restored by Tricia
Foley, a designer and author, features snowy white
walls and upholstery, exposed beams, and a
fireplace Foley framed in a refined wainscot inspired
by a Colonial Williamsburg architectural detail.

ABOVE
Fashion designer/decorator/author Michael
Leva created a serene setting at his 1765
saltbox in Litchfield County, Connecticut; the
1970s sofa is upholstered in a Clarence House
mohair, the painted side chair is 1920s
French, and the lamp is made from a vintage
pharmacy bottle filled with colored water.

ABOVE
The drawing room at Glen Feshie
Lodge, a Scottish Highlands
castle decorated by Ward Denton and
Christopher Gardner of Denton & Gardner,
features a cache of pillows
covered in antique tartans; the 19th-century
Persian carpet is layered atop
rush matting.

RIGHT
For a Paris client's bachelor pad, designer
Bruno de Caumont assembled
a quirky mix of antiques and flea-market oddities,
including Chinese scrolls and Empire and
Louis XIII–style furniture.

OPPOSITE
Photographer Pieter Estersohn evoked
the feeling of a 1920s Paris atelier
at his Gramercy Park duplex penthouse
with vintage furnishings—
including a Jean Prouvé daybed and
Jacques Adnet armchair—and wall-to-wall
Brancusi-like bookcases of
his own design; antique mosque lamps are
suspended from the skylight.

"I WANT EVERY ROOM
TO FEEL LIKE I'M JOURNEYING TO A NEW PLACE"
— *Jeff Klein,*
restaurateur/hotelier

ABOVE
At her fanciful Manhattan lair, globe-trotting
photographer Calliope conjured an exotic corner
with stenciled walls and a low slipcovered
banquette layered with hand-blocked bolsters
and antique embroidered pillows.

RIGHT
The fireplace surround in the living room at Dar Es
Saada, the Marrakech guesthouse of fashion designer Yves Saint Laurent and his partner Pierre Bergé,
was created by American-born designer Bill Willis and
inlaid with tile from Fez; the cocktail table is by
Jean Dunand, and the chair in the foreground is Syrian.

OPPOSITE
Rustic stone floors at
the Bedford, New York, estate of Stephen
Sills and James Huniford of
Stephen Sills Associates provide a foil for antiques
of various periods and provenance:
A William and Mary seat is upholstered in a
Venetian velvet stripe, the 18th-century
Italian armchair is covered in a paisley-blocked cotton,
and the settee and chair in the foreground
are French Régence.

RIGHT
A luxurious overscale
banquette in the three-story living room
of nightclub impresario Jaouad Kadiri's
Marrakech house is anchored by
Uzbek-inspired tilework; the
pillows are covered in sari silks, and
the English-style armchairs
are upholstered in vintage Persian rugs.

BELOW
The Paris living room of designers
Dimonah and Mehmet Iksel,
housed in an 18th-century building in the
2nd arrondissement, doubles as a showroom
for Iksel Decorative Arts, their
line of exotic wall coverings and panels.
The couple created the gilded
cocktail table based on a centuries-old Persian
astrological motif, and the
curtains are of a Rubelli silk.

OPPOSITE
The Manhattan drawing room of costume-jewelry
designer Kenneth Jay Lane reflects his
wide-ranging interests;
plush ottomans, animal prints, and
Persian carpets hold sway amid a 19th-century
English Regency table and
needlework-covered Louis XV chairs.

TOP RIGHT
A Han dynasty horse is displayed
in the Paris living room of fashion designer/decorator
Rose Anne de Pampelonne; antique side
chairs are upholstered in a zebra-stripe silk velvet, and
custom-made bookcases hold false volumes
whose titles refer to family members.

BOTTOM RIGHT
Designer Eric Cohler suspended
paintings in front of the double-height windows
of his New York City duplex; the club
chairs and the George II chair are covered
in fabrics from Lee Jofa, and the
rug is by Asha Carpets.

BELOW
Claire Cormier-Fauvel created the
bejeweled ship chandelier in interior decorator
Muriel Brandolini's Upper East Side
living room; the sofa is 19th century, and the Smarties
cocktail table is by Mattia Bonetti.

OPPOSITE
A dilapidated 19th-century
creamery and barn in Millbrook, New York,
were transformed by jewelry
designer Mish Tworkowski and architect Joseph
Singer into an urbane retreat. The
living room's antique étagères are French;
Christopher Spitzmiller
crafted the Aurora Double-Gourd lamps.

ABOVE
The living room at the Sharon,
Connecticut, getaway of
accessories designers Richard Lambertson
and John Truex features a tailored assortment
of antique and vintage pieces, including
slipper chairs covered in an Italian
awning-stripe cotton and a 19th-century
English overmantel mirror.

LEFT
A sitting room at decorator
Chessy Rayner's Southampton, New York,
home is furnished with vintage wicker and
Anglo-Indian caned armchairs; pristine white walls
and a pair of hibiscus standards lend an air
of laid-back elegance.

ABOVE
A charming amalgam of antique
French chairs, flea-market finds, and casual
cotton upholstery fits the bill
at the Water Mill, New York, home
of designer Gary Guerrette and his partner,
Tom Lawson; a palampore from India
is displayed above the sofa.

RIGHT
Decorator Tom Scheerer created
an airy setting for clients in Jupiter Island,
Florida; an overscale chandelier is
the focal point of the
double-height living room, where
sunlight is filtered through
carved-wood shutters from India.

OPPOSITE
In Amagansett, New York, decorator
John Stedila conjured a sophisticated beach
retreat from a former fire station;
the living room features an
18th-century French settee upholstered
in a ticking stripe, a vintage garden
chair, and a dramatic blue-lacquer screen
of Stedila's design.

OPPOSITE
Architect Orlando Diaz-Azcuy's
San Francisco home is a study of old and new:
Reproduction Piranesi urns from
Soane flank a window in the living room,
where a white-lacquer
center table anchors the space; pickled-fir
brackets from a 15th-century convent
grace the double-height
ceiling, and the dark-stained floors
are hand-planed.

RIGHT
At the New York City apartment
of decorating team Edward Zajac and Richard
Callahan, a pair of 18th-century
Russian chairs provides
balance to a room notable for its profusion
of pattern and detail; the ornate
Line Vautrin–inspired
mirrors were crafted by Zajac.

BELOW
Near the Elysée Palace in Paris,
the apartment of Inès de la Fressange—fashion
designer, model, and muse—has
the feeling of a Swedish summer house, with a
pale-blue-gray Gustavian palette,
cotton fabrics in stripes and
checks, slipcovered Louis XVI furniture,
and painted park chairs.

PRECEDING PAGES
A steel-and-glass structure that architect
Sean McEvoy added to his rooftop flat offers unobstructed
views of Paris; the raised floor is waxed concrete,
and the 1950s chairs are by Pierre Paulin for Thonet.

OPPOSITE
In Anne and Tony Fisher's refined Upper East Side
townhouse, decorated by Tom Fox and Joe Nahem of Fox-
Nahem Design, an 18th-century Italian chandelier
hangs above a pair of tufted chairs by William Haines; the
cocktail table is by Diego Giacometti, and the
artwork is by Ed Ruscha.

ABOVE
Glamour gets a mod update at designer Larry Laslo's Manhattan townhouse, where furnishings from his collection
for Directional complement soaring double-height ceilings.

TOP RIGHT
Couturiers Mark Badgley and James Mischka of Badgley
Mischka embrace a graphic black-and-white
palette at their Greenwich Village duplex; Mischka coated the
furniture in layers of glossy paint, the sofa is covered in pet-
friendly white vinyl, and accessories in silver, mercury glass, and
crystal add sparkle and gleam.

RIGHT
An Arne Jacobsen Swan chair upholstered in
mink takes center stage at the Manhattan apartment of fashion
designer Gilles Mendel; the bold cocktail table and Leleu-style
armchairs were designed by Alan Tanksley.

ABOVE
Fashion designer Zang Toi salutes France in his Upper East Side
apartment with a suite of Louis XVI Revival furniture upholstered in Loro Piana
cashmere and a pair of Natasha Zupan's overscale portraits
of Marie Antoinette. Toi lacquered the walls and floors—even the antique
furniture—in glossy enamel; the rug is silver fox.

RIGHT
Ellsworth Kelly's *Black/White* punctuates a creamy living room
designed by Michael S. Smith for Lynn Forester de Rothschild and her husband,
Sir Evelyn de Rothschild, in Manhattan. The sofa
and Bridgewater chairs are by Jonas
Upholstery, and the antique Persian Khorasan carpet is
from Beauvais Carpets.

OPPOSITE
In a loftlike aerie in Manhattan's
Museum Tower, John Demsey, group president of
Estée Lauder Companies, displays
a collection of black-and-white fashion and
paparazzi photos; the cocktail
table is by Christian Liaigre from Holly
Hunt, the sculpture is by Kenneth Snelson,
and the rug is by Carini Lang.

RIGHT
Carlos Souza, jewelry
designer and longtime Valentino public-relations
powerhouse, mixed iconic
midcentury-modern pieces with a deft
hand at his Rome apartment,
including a Mies van der Rohe leather
daybed and ottomans, a Noguchi paper
floor lamp, and artworks
by Gary Hume and James Brown.

BELOW
Flos's sculptural Arco lamp, a James
Nares painting, and a wood
totem add an eclectic touch to the
linear layout of advertising/marketing executive
Kim Vernon's Manhattan living
room; the wool-and-silk rug is by
Calvin Klein Home.

"COLOR IS THE
GREATEST WAY TO CONVEY PERSONALITY"
— *Steven Gambrel, interior designer*

LEFT
Decorator Muriel Brandolini brought colorful
exuberance to a client's glass-and-steel Hudson
Valley house, which was designed by architect
Thomas Phifer; the sofas are upholstered in
a Lulu DK fabric, the cocktail table is by Albrizzi,
and the rug is by AM Collections.

ABOVE
The living room of a turn-of-the-century Manhattan
townhouse decorated by architect Lee F. Mindel
of Shelton, Mindel & Associates features a set
of circa-1925 French armchairs and an English Regency
chaise; the artwork is by Günther Förg.

> "IN THE MOST SUCCESSFUL
> SPACES, YOU DON'T
> SEE EVERYTHING AT ONCE. THE MORE TIME
> YOU SPEND IN THEM, THE
> MORE YOU DISCOVER. THEY OPEN UP
> LIKE FLOWERS"
> — *Vicente Wolf, interior designer*

ABOVE
In the Southampton, New York, living room of Reed Krakoff, president and executive creative director of Coach, and his decorator wife, Delphine, the sofa is flanked by 1940s armchairs, and the throw pillows are covered in Pucci scarves. The paintings are by Ludwig Sander, the Ring cocktail table is a Garouste and Bonetti design, and the ostrich sculpture is by Diego Giacometti.

RIGHT
Decorator Victoria Hagan used a classic seaside palette of blue and white in a client's Bridgehampton, New York, living room. She designed the overscale white-lacquer table, and the sofas are covered in cobalt linen; an antique dhurrie plays on the nautical theme.

ABOVE
The living room of Cathy and Marc Lasry's
Upper East Side townhouse,
decorated by DD Allen of Pierce Allen,
features an adroit mix of
French and English antiques and
modern furnishings.

RIGHT
Laura Henson called on her
son decorator J. Randall Powers
for help with her Houston high-rise
living room. He designed the
cocktail table and parchment-covered
cabinet; the low side table is 1920s
Jean-Michel Frank.

OPPOSITE
In the London apartment of jewelry
designer Fruzsina Keehn, which
was decorated in collaboration with Alex
Papachristidis, a silk-velvet sofa
adapted from a 1940s Jean-Charles Moreux design
is flanked by a pair of Russian Empire–style
chairs and antique gilt-wood
sconces. The nude studies were found
in a Vermont antiques shop,
and the floor lamp and cocktail table
are vintage Baguès.

OPPOSITE
The Manhattan living
room of interior designer Bunny Williams
showcases a shortlist of her passions,
from garden-themed
objects to worldly antiques.

ABOVE
Decorator Kerry Joyce created
a serene setting in the
Beverly Hills home of actress Jami Gertz
and her husband, Tony Ressler;
for a subtle look, the sofas
are slipcovered using the reverse side
of a vibrant Pierre Frey cotton.

RIGHT
For clients in Quogue,
New York, interior designer Mark Hampton
commissioned the painting
of a faux-marble motif on the floor
of a sitting area.

STYLE GUIDE

■ The best interiors are created over time and don't look as if their furnishings were all purchased at the same store. Intriguing rooms—spaces where you want to linger—feature the contrasts of old and new, smooth and rough textures, and a mix of both grand and humble objects and materials.

■ A sofa doesn't have to be flanked by matching end tables. Why not place a small stylish chest of drawers at one end and sculptural nesting tables at the other? Similarly, a cocktail table can be a group of diminutive tables, an upholstered ottoman topped with a tray, or a narrow bench—let your imagination lead the way. Oval or circular shapes will help break up a boxy room, and a table with a shelf offers another surface to stow books and magazines.

■ Consider the quality of light as well as its comfort level when developing the decorating scheme of your living room. Gentle pools of light from lamps are usually more welcoming—and flattering—than the allover illumination cast by a chandelier.

■ Be thoughtful. No guest should be marooned sitting in the shadows and clutching a cocktail all night: Every sofa or chair needs a source of light and a place to set down a drink or a book.

■ If you crave a soigné living room but lack the resources for no-holds-barred glamour, remember it's often little touches that make a big difference. Dress up a nondescript sofa with pillows fashioned from silk scarves or chic fabric remnants; layer a cashmere throw or antique textile over a seat back or arm. Upgrade a favorite chair by restuffing its cushion with luxurious down. And fresh flowers never fail to make a room more elegant and inviting.

LEFT
In the Westchester County,
New York, home of Ralph Pucci of Ralph Pucci
International and his wife, Ann, decorator
Vicente Wolf used a single color—brown—and
manipulated it into an essay on tones. The
painting is by Bodo Korsig, and the sofas, armchairs,
and cocktail table are Wolf designs.

LIBRARIES &
HOME OFFICES

Though featherweight laptops and personal communications devices have made the world one big office, no house can do without a dedicated spot for dashing off a quick letter or monitoring one's online interests, from banking to auctions to breaking news. Which explains why libraries and home offices remain essential components of many people's daily lives. Some of these rooms are large enough to combine the best attributes of both spaces into one restful, finely appointed chamber, with floor-to-ceiling shelves for storing well-thumbed volumes and back issues of favorite magazines, plump sofas and beckoning chairs, and a desk or table at the ready for lengthy periods of work. Most, however, are much smaller in size yet can be just as thoughtfully designed, smartly tucked into a corner of a bedroom or occupying a reappropriated closet garnished with cubbyholes, shelves, and file drawers. Novelist and tastemaker Edith Wharton noted in her groundbreaking 1897 book *The Decoration of Houses* that work spaces, grand or modest, should be planned with practical considerations firmly in mind, meaning knickknacks and photographs ought to be few and surfaces "large, substantial, and clear of everything but lamps, books, and papers." Sensibly written and duly noted. But regardless of scale, libraries and home offices can be models of efficiency and still pack a glamorous punch. Organize your work space by placing papers in linen-covered file boxes. Brighten bookcases by enlivening the backs of their shelves with a graphic fabric, fantastical wallpaper, or a vibrant paint color or crowning them with an impressive assortment of blue-and-white ceramic vases and ginger jars. Rolling ladders of traditional wood or modern enameled metal allow easy access to out-of-reach shelves while lending an atmosphere of scholarship. While it is true that books do furnish a room, as the adage goes, it takes a lot more to make a home office do its job and be inspiring too. ■

"I MUST HAVE
BOOKS EVERYWHERE.
THEY'RE THE SOUL
OF A ROOM—THEY REVEAL THE TASTE,
THE INTERESTS, AND
THE SECRETS OF WHOEVER
LIVES THERE"

— *Diane von Furstenberg,*
fashion designer

PRECEDING PAGES
A corner of decorator Charlotte Moss's living room
at her East Hampton, New York, retreat features built-in
bookcases accessed by a rolling ladder; Moss bound
archival issues of favorite magazines in leather.

LEFT
Stacks of books teeter in the Upper East Side study of dealer
extraordinaire Roger Prigent of Malmaison Antiques; an
18th-century candelabra sits on a neoclassical table, and a collection
of French and American tea and coffee urns lines the redbrick wall.

ABOVE
The Manhattan dressing room of fashion journalist Amy
Fine Collins does double duty as an office; her
Louis XV–style desk once belonged to Hugh Hefner, and artwork
by friends including Robert Couturier, Gene Meyer, Karl
Lagerfeld, and Victor Skrebneski is displayed on the walls.

OPPOSITE
An oversize bulletin board in designer Thomas O'Brien's New York City apartment serves as a wall of inspiration; the folding library ladder is from Aero, his SoHo shop, and the Bennett storage boxes are from his line for Hickory Chair.

RIGHT
In the study of a Manhattan apartment owned by color-loving clients, decorator Katie Ridder complemented custom-made floor-to-ceiling bookshelves with a grid wall treatment of lilac-hued Edelman leather.

BELOW
Thomas O'Brien in his loftlike double-height living room, which functions as a living/sleeping/dining and home-office space; the former bedroom is now a study and dressing room.

TOP LEFT
At the London apartment of Jimmy Choo
founder Tamara Mellon, decorator
Martyn Lawrence-Bullard mixed a vintage Jansen desk, a 1960s
Eames chair upholstered in hot-pink leather,
and a Warhol print of Grace Kelly.

CENTER LEFT
Antiques dealer Aline Chastel of Galerie
Chastel-Maréchal in Paris works at home at a curvaceous
vintage writing table; the lamp is by André Arbus.

ABOVE
One wall of fashion designer Ralph Rucci's
dining room has towering bronze-and-leather étagères
stacked with books; 19th-century scholar's chairs are
pulled up to a bronze tree table, and
the Chinese stone torso dates from the 6th century.

LEFT
The focal point of architect Gil Schafer's attic
studio in Dutchess County, New York, is a neoclassical window;
the floor lamp is a retooled surveyor's tripod.

OPPOSITE
The late-18th-century home of Kate and Jim Lehrer in
West Virginia, restored by architect Hugh
Newell Jacobsen, features a striking Hepplewhite-style
desk designed by Jacobsen.

OPPOSITE
Matching Eames chairs finish a
sleek study architect
Peter Pawlak devised for the Manhattan
loft of Bottega Veneta executive
Lisa Pomerantz and her
family; the woven-leather satchel is
by Bottega Veneta.

ABOVE
Hundreds of books and magazines
created by design legends
Lella and Massimo Vignelli are displayed on the
shelves of the couple's Manhattan
library; their Ara chair was inspired by the
work of Frank Lloyd Wright
and Charles Rennie Mackintosh.

RIGHT
In the Beverly Hills home of
entertainment executive
Lisa Henson, designed by Madeline Stuart,
Darren Waterston's painting
Moisture Seekers serves as a backdrop for a
Chinese desk and chair
and a Tiffany-style claw-foot lamp.

ABOVE
Simple pine shelves are punctuated
by 18th-century mahogany
pilasters at art-and-antiques dealer Pierre Passebon's
French-countryside retreat,
which was decorated by Jacques Grange;
a frieze of antique tiles draws
the eye to the ceiling.

RIGHT
Designer Matthew Patrick Smyth
added a graceful note
to the library of his 19th-century Colonial in
Sharon, Connecticut, with a vintage
French desk from Neo-Studio.

OPPOSITE
In their Brooklyn library, artists
Vik Muniz and Janaina Tschäpe installed
custom-made shelving, vintage
industrial hanging light fixtures, and carpet panels
by Flor; the mobile sculpture
is by Man Ray, and the steel chair
is a Ron Arad design.

TOP LEFT
Entrepreneur Will Kopelman's
West Hollywood loft features a mezzanine home
office, where he works at a desk
purchased in the 1960s by his father, Arie L. Kopelman;
the wire chairs are classic Bertoia.

ABOVE
The sculptural vintage desk
and Belgian chair in the Greenwich Village apartment
of master hairstylist John Barrett
were bought at an
auction benefit for Housing Works.

LEFT
Decorator Nate Berkus
preserved the original silver-leaf wall covering
found in his Chicago apartment;
its subtle patina contrasts with an angular
desk and chair and bold striped rug.

OPPOSITE
In Brentwood, California,
interior designer Michael S. Smith uses a vintage
Gio Ponti glass-top table as his desk.

OPPOSITE
Public-relations executive Mike Clifford
brought drama to the library he created in the entry
of his Hollywood Hills house by painting the
walls backing the bookcases in a Farrow & Ball red.

TOP RIGHT
Novelist Bret Easton Ellis and his interior designer
Susan Forristal at the writer's apartment
near Union Square in New York City; the bed, bedside
consoles, and mazelike bookshelves
are by Reed Karen.

CENTER RIGHT
Pooches Leo and Seymour at rest in
the office area of artist Anne Becker's loft in
Manhattan's Alphabet City;
a French farm table serves as a desk.

BOTTOM RIGHT
A singular mix of objects and vintage furnishings is
displayed at the Southampton, New York, weekend house
of philanthropist Beth Rudin DeWoody.

BELOW
At a client's West Village penthouse,
designer Steven Gambrel installed wall-to-wall shelves
connected by narrow metal rods;
the stacked boxes are covered in linen.

STYLE GUIDE

■ Equip your library or home office with a luxurious daybed or convertible sofa so the area can do double duty as a guest room. And remember, an office needn't look corporate: Display artwork, an inspiration board, and personal objects to make the space more individual.

■ Whether you work at home or bring projects home from the office, invest in a surface with space to spread out, and don't skimp on great lighting. Also, the chair you use most often should be comfortable for extended periods of time, if not actually ergonomic. A well-cushioned antique chair is a terrific juxtaposition in a sleek contemporary setting, while a modern seat can add the perfect idiosyncratic touch to a classic room.

■ Dedicated readers no doubt have shelves filled to overflowing with masses of beloved volumes, but even if most of your reading is done online, books make attractive and engaging decor and add a sense of warmth and history to a space. Why not spend an afternoon in the sale stacks at a secondhand book shop and pick well-worn hardcovers that look appealing and whose subject matter will invite guests to take them down? Start your library with fiction classics—Hemingway, Faulkner, and Fitzgerald, for instance—and remove the dust jackets to uncover their colorful spines. Or display collections in your bookcases—from seashells to family photographs to vintage Murano glass.

■ Think smart: Libraries and home offices are by definition repositories for books and files, so develop a storage scheme that keeps the materials you use most within easy reach. In addition to accommodating the volumes and papers you already have, plan for those the future will undoubtedly bring. Adjustable shelves are key for space-conscious placement, and bookcases with cabinets below offer more storage options.

■ Most file cabinets have no style, so hide them in a closet or tucked under a desk. Worthy alternatives are decorative containers such as wicker baskets or sturdy stackable boxes wrapped in chic linen or wallpaper that complements the decor of the room. Or have a carpenter construct built-in file drawers for a tailor-made space with seamless good looks.

LEFT
The millwork and architectural detail
in the double-height library
at Villa Vistorta, the Brandolini-family estate in Italy's
Veneto region that was decorated by
Renzo Mongiardino, are painted in Biedermeier-
style trompe l'oeil.

DINING ROOMS

A dining room is more than a space for consuming daily meals solo, *en famille,* or in party mode. Its bottom-line furnishings are bare-bones in number when compared to other rooms in the house—nothing more than a table, chairs, and perhaps a sideboard or console for serving—but a dining room offers an extraordinary chance to make a spectacular statement, whether your favored cuisine is home-delivered Cantonese noodles or home-cooked chicken Cordon Bleu. And why not? "Eating is really one of your indoor sports," larger-than-life designer Dorothy Draper wrote in her effervescent 1939 lifestyle manual *Decorating Is Fun!* "You play three times a day, and it's well worth while to make the game as pleasant as possible." Just get the basics in place before masterminding the drama. Chairs should be agreeably firm, so if they are wood or another hard material, provide a cushion. The table should be a sensible height and have enough legroom, so test it with two or more people to ensure it makes every guest comfortable. A dining room's lighting ought to be adjustable, because not every meal will have the same mood or character. Candles in a chandelier or on the table cast the most flattering glow—deploy enough so you can see what's on your plate, and make sure they are both unscented and dripless—but a dimmable ceiling fixture or sconces will also do the trick nicely. As for the decor, anything goes: Antiquarian formal, mismatched casual, or lacquered ultramod, all that really matters is that the environment is invigorating. Lavish the windows with sweeps of silk taffeta, or leave them undressed so sunlight bathes the room in the manner of a Vermeer painting. Sheathe the walls in paper depicting a chinoiserie garden, or paint them snow-white to throw finely polished antiques into high relief. And don't forget, a dining room doesn't have to be limited to a single purpose—fill it with bookcases, for instance, and you've got a room that serves as a library by day and party central when night falls. ■

PRECEDING PAGES
Decorator Bunny Williams crafted a
razzle-dazzle dining room for Park Avenue
clients using a mirror based on a
William Kent design and a kilim by Allegra Hicks.

OPPOSITE
In Jamie Creel and Marco
Scarani's round periwinkle-blue dining
room in Paris, Thomas Boog's
cast-iron Coral chandelier dangles over
a vintage Serge Roche table.

RIGHT
Not far from Paris, the formality of
the Dutch Dining Room
in the historic Château de Groussay—
which was restored by media entrepreneur
Jean-Louis Remilleux—
contrasts with side chairs charmingly
slipcovered in cotton checks.

BELOW
A Left Bank dining room,
decorated for a client by antiques dealers
Françoise and Yves Gastou, features
a Venetian-glass chandelier and candleholders
and a striking Gilbert Poillerat dining
table with a wood
top lacquered bottle-green.

OPPOSITE
Designer Miles Redd sheathed Mila and Tom Tuttle's
Manhattan dining room in De Gournay's
Sans Souci wall covering and commandeered a
vintage suzani for use as a tablecloth.

ABOVE
In the Amagansett, New York, dining room of
Luigi Caiola and Sean McGill, Joe Nahem of Fox-Nahem Design
paired 1940s chairs with a sculptural Italian table;
the fireplace is inset with 19th-century
Portuguese tiles from Solar Antique Tiles, and
the wallpaper is by Zoffany.

TOP RIGHT
Lorraine and Patrick Frey set a lively mood
in their Paris dining room with a quirky Zettel'z
chandelier by Ingo Maurer, furniture by
Philippe Hurel, and curtain and wall-upholstery fabrics
by their family firm, Pierre Frey.

RIGHT
Anthropologie president Glen Senk and the
firm's antiques buyer, Keith Johnson, grouped historic
pieces—mismatched chairs and a long
tufted-leather settee—in their Philadelphia dining
room; 19th-century street lanterns are
installed above the 1860s mahogany table.

PRECEDING PAGES
Romantic flowers, rustic carved-wood chairs, and a
19th-century trestle table that seats 14 evoke a European sensibility in
the outdoor dining area of Madonna's Beverly Hills home.

OPPOSITE
Understated elegance rules in the breakfast room
of decorator Darryl Carter's retreat in the Plains, Virginia; open
shelves display pristine white tableware, the
English daybed and tooled-leather chair are antique, and the
rough-hewn farm table is a Carter design.

ABOVE
At the Millbrook, New York, weekend house of
Frédéric Fekkai and Shirin von Wulffen, designed by Selina van der
Geest, the kitchen opens onto a breakfast room with
exposed beams, industrial-style metal chairs ordered from the
Sundance Catalog, and a table set with English ironstone.

TOP RIGHT
An antique dressmaker's table from Argentina
stands at the ready in the 1770 Dutchess County, New York,
farmhouse designer Edwina Hunt shares
with her young family; the woven-hide chairs and candlesticks of
bone and ram's horn are from Hunt's eponymous
home-furnishings line.

RIGHT
The quiet simplicity of Hans J. Wegner Wishbone chairs,
a foursquare table, and framed insect specimens in
the Bellport, New York, dining room of architect Tim Furzer
and Calvin Klein creative director Kevin Carrigan
belies the exuberance of the couple's parties; the
ceramics are by Calvin Klein Home.

"THERE'S NOTHING I CAN'T
LIVE WITHOUT, BUT
THERE ARE THINGS AND MEMORIES THAT
ARE DEAR TO ME"

— *Albert Hadley, interior designer*

ABOVE
The chocolate-brown dining room at decorator
Albert Hadley's Connecticut house features a
19th-century mahogany dining table surrounded
by a set of early-20th-century Louis XVI–style
chairs commissioned by architect Ogden
Codman; the hanging lamp is a Hadley design.

RIGHT
The Majorca dining room of art dealer Hans
Neuendorf, designed by architect
Claudio Silvestrin, is rigorously minimal, with a
stone floor, massive travertine table, and
Hans J. Wegner's curvilinear Wishbone chairs.

OPPOSITE
Donatella Versace's Milan dining
room pays tribute to
her love of ornamentation: The Venetian
chandelier is late 16th century, the
chairs are early-19th-century French,
the tableware is by Versace for
Rosenthal, and the murals
echo her collection of Japanese
and Chinese porcelain.

TOP RIGHT
The San Francisco dining room
of decorators Jeffry Weisman and Andrew
Fisher of Fisher Weisman showcases
a lyrical table of their own
design and a shell-encrusted chandelier
handcrafted by Fisher.

BOTTOM RIGHT
A 1940s cabinet from Amy Perlin
Antiques holds pride of place in Pamela and
Roger Birnbaum's Beverly Hills dining room, which
was decorated by Michael S. Smith;
a 1927 Vittorio Zecchini chandelier is reflected
in the mirrored niche.

BELOW
Interior designer Kerry Joyce
added distinctive detailing to the Beverly
Hills dining room of actress
Jami Gertz and her husband, Tony Ressler,
with gold-leafed ovals applied to the
wall above the dado.

ABOVE
The Manhattan dining area of songwriters
Marc Shaiman and Scott Wittman, decorated by Eric
Hughes, is no less spirited than their
Tony-award-winning work; a shimmering 1970s
Paco Rabanne screen is displayed on the wall, and the
chairs are covered in a Lulu DK flame-stitch fabric.

RIGHT
In the Tribeca loft shared by decorator
Christopher Coleman and fashion designer Angel Sanchez,
a Flos lamp is mounted above a sleek stainless-steel
table and Lucite bench.

OPPOSITE
Boston interior designer Frank Roop and his wife,
Sharon, entertain guests at a T. H. Robsjohn-Gibbings walnut
table with Danish chairs; the wall sculpture is by
Curtis Jeré, the light fixture is by
Fortuny, and the floating bookshelves
are a Roop trademark.

TOP LEFT
The refined aesthetic of fashion designer
Josie Natori and her husband,
Ken, is reflected in their Upper East Side
dining room, designed by architect Calvin Tsao;
an antique Chinese textile is displayed above
the sideboard, Tang dynasty figurines
serve as centerpieces, and
the table and chairs are by Tsao.

BOTTOM LEFT
Designer Muriel Brandolini applied silk
hand-embroidered in Vietnam to the dining room
walls of the Manhattan townhouse she
shares with her husband, Nuno, and their children; the
Martin Szekely table is from Galerie
Kreo, and the Louis XV–style chairs are antique.

BELOW
Tastemaker Lee Radziwill's New York City
dining room is sheathed in a vibrant
Milanese silk stripe; the chairs are 19th century.

OPPOSITE
It's full-on drama in a dining room decorator
Brian McCarthy lacquered persimmon for a client; the table
is George II, and the sisal is by Stark.

"WHEN MY DINING ROOM IS
FILLED WITH PEOPLE, THEY BECOME PIECES
OF ART THAT MAKE
IT EVEN MORE BEAUTIFUL"
— *Sarah Jessica Parker, actor*

ABOVE
On the isle of Lamu, off the coast of Kenya,
designer Marie-Paule Pellé fashioned
an exotic dining room with a chandelier
from Turkey and ebony chairs created
by local craftspeople; the dining
table is a retrofitted century-old bed.

RIGHT
A collection of plates made for use
on Turkish ships is displayed on a clean-cut
fireplace surround at Mica and
Ahmet Ertegün's house in Bodrum, Turkey.

Brice Marden's *Blue Horizontal* forms a
modernist backdrop in a dining room designed by David
Kleinberg for Manhattan clients.

CENTER LEFT
The London dining room of the Rug Company
founders Suzanne and Christopher Sharp pairs a chandelier
found at a Cairo souk with an heirloom oak table.

ABOVE
At a Bridgehampton, New York, home
decorated by Eric Hughes for Sarah Jessica Parker and
Matthew Broderick, a motley collection of
chairs received a unifying coat of matte black paint; the table is by
Hughes, and the antique chandelier is Egyptian.

LEFT
Architect Hugh Newell Jacobsen used his
signature egg-crate bookshelves to give Eugenie Voorhees's
Nantucket dining room a library feel.

OPPOSITE
Designer Kristiina Ratia juxtaposed an antique
chandelier with a side chair by Ralph Lauren Home covered
in a snappy awning stripe at her Connecticut home.

"WHEN I
ENTERTAIN AT HOME, I TAKE
TIME AND PLEASURE IN
THE SMALL DETAILS THAT MAKE ALL
THE DIFFERENCE.
ENTERTAINING IS ABOUT
GIVING TO PEOPLE AND SHARING
WITH THEM"

— *Valentino, couturier*

LEFT
Jacqueline Coumans of Le Décor Français used
a lilac-bedecked cotton with cheerful
abandon in her Southampton, New York, dining
room, upholstering the walls as well as
the banquette; the chairs are flea-market finds,
and the cushions are made of vintage fabrics.

ABOVE
Fashion designer Cynthia Rowley created
a fanciful wall covering for the dining area of the
downtown Manhattan townhouse she shares
with her husband, Bill Powers, and their
daughters; the side chairs and banquette are
covered in a Cole & Son cotton.

OPPOSITE
A fleet of André Arbus iron chairs is grouped around a lacquer table in the dining area of Luigi Caiola and Sean McGill's Manhattan duplex, decorated by Fox-Nahem Design; the Line Vautrin mirror is from the 1930s.

ABOVE
Jeffrey Bilhuber painted a dining room cool lavender for London-based American clients; the table is paired with a curved sofa and two sets of chairs to lessen the formality of the space.

LEFT
The tangerine dining room decorator Steven Gambrel put together for John Rolfes's Hamptons cottage looks sun-splashed even in stormy weather; the 1940s table is from R. E. Steele Antiques.

OPPOSITE
Dark wood strikes a moody note in
designer Lisa Jackson's Upper East Side dining room;
the hanging fixture was
fashioned from three vintage Baguès lanterns.

ABOVE
Smoky blue linen curtains add soft color to decorator
Nate Berkus's Chicago dining area; the
chandelier is Italian, the chairs are cerused oak, and the pedestal
table is a Berkus design.

LEFT
Bottega Veneta executive Lisa Pomerantz paired
Hans J. Wegner Wishbone chairs with a Scott Jordan table at her
family's Manhattan loft; the Prouvé-
inspired shelving is by Peter Pawlak Design Studio.

STYLE GUIDE

■ The dining room is used less frequently than other rooms in your home, so it's the perfect place to be adventurous, especially if you're typically timid about paint and pattern but are ready for a change. Experiment with deep, saturated color on the walls or cover them with an intriguing fabric or wallpaper. Display a large abstract canvas, silver-leaf the ceiling, or hang a glittery light fixture. After all, this is a space for entertaining, so why hold back?

■ Dining tables are usually 29 or 30 inches tall, so dining seats should be 17 to 18 inches high; don't be afraid to contrast modern pieces with antiques or to mix the styles of chairs used. Mismatched seating makes a room less stuffy, and replacing a row of chairs with an upholstered bench or settee is a refreshing change.

■ A single dining table is usually sufficient for most hosts, but why stick to the tried and true? Two round tables that seat four to six people each are a lively alternative.

■ Few things fill a dinner guest with more angst than a chair that wiggles and creaks, so avoid delicate antiques. If your table can accommodate them, armchairs up the comfort ante, but be sure to spread them around; their traditional placement at the ends of the table usually guarantees it's the hosts' seats that are the most inviting.

■ Whether it is a neoclassical tureen, a profusion of orchids, or a bowl laden with bounty from the farmer's market, a centerpiece makes your table look fully dressed. But check that diners can see each other—the decor should be an accent, not a blockade. Small potted flowers or groupings of vases designed for a single bloom are also stylish options.

■ Dining rooms needn't be formal: Create a carefree, casual vibe by layering exotic throws or coverlets atop tablecloths, and fearlessly mix silver, glass, and china patterns—just have fun. Table settings are memorable when they're bold, not boring.

LEFT
In a dining room in France, a Chinese-red
banquette and khaki-green walls
set off a framed series of turn-of-the-century
photos by Robert Demachy.

KITCHENS

"The grand thing about cooking is that you can eat your mistakes," culinary guru Julia Child once said. But errors in kitchen planning are harder to swallow. Intelligent organization, copious storage, sufficient counter space, appliances that suit your needs—these elements require careful attention. Once those issues have been addressed, make sure they are incorporated into a kitchen that looks as good as it cooks. For many people, this means a place with a nostalgic feel—it is a room we have potent childhood memories of, after all. But modern kitchens have their own magnetic pull, especially when a laboratory-like space with clinical countertops and cabinetry incorporates a dose of warmth via a wall of windows to let in natural light or a wood floor whose weathered planks tone down the futuristic chic. In either setting, let art climb to the ceiling. Some of our favorite kitchens showcase, for instance, quirky framed paintings of earthenware pitchers, cutting-edge contemporary photography, quiet still lifes depicting the bounty of a harvest, and sleek pieces of glassware displayed like museum acquisitions. Or try a jolt of unexpected color—from a fire-engine-red wall treatment to bold cerulean tilework—to give your kitchen pizzazz. Open shelving works well in both traditional and modernist schemes—stacks of white restaurant-quality china are as appealing to look at as rows of venerable porcelain. (Consider closed cabinets, however, if dust is a concern.) You might crave an immense island with a second sink and loads of extra storage, or you could be happy with a large table at the center of the room as an earthy prep station that, with little more than a wipe and a jug of flowers, can be transformed into a casually elegant dining spot. Built-in lacquer cabinetry supplies cosmopolitan style, or you can conjure a gemütlich atmosphere with a hefty farm sink and mismatched freestanding furniture such as breakfronts and carved tables that seem to have been amassed over generations. Remember that even if you rarely cook, the kitchen is so often the room where guests naturally flock during a party, so make it a reflection of your personal style as much as your more formal spaces. ■

PRECEDING PAGES
The Tribeca kitchen of Alfredo Paredes, executive
vice president of global creative services at Polo Ralph Lauren, and Brad
Goldfarb, a magazine editor, is a model of efficiency
with open shelving, stainless-steel industrial cabinets and counters,
and sleek appliances by Viking and Sub-Zero.

OPPOSITE
In Goshen, New York, accessories designers
Richard Lambertson and John Truex showcase a charmingly
haphazard display of framed oil
studies in a kitchen with soaring 25-foot ceilings.

ABOVE
Rosy hues prevail in the London kitchen of the Rug Company's
Christopher and Suzanne Sharp, shown with their
morning coffee; the Roman blinds are of a Cath Kidston floral,
and the Chinese lantern was bought in SoHo,
near their Manhattan shop.

LEFT
Designer Lorraine Kirke painted the metal kitchen cabinets
in her family's apartment near New York City's
Washington Square "Valentine's Day–red" to contrast
with the checkerboard floor.

OPPOSITE
Anthropologie's president, Glen Senk, and the firm's antiques buyer,
Keith Johnson, created a European-style unfitted kitchen for
their Philadelphia home; the oak-and-marble island is a replica of one at La Mirande hotel in
Avignon, and the vintage grape-collecting basket is from the Champagne valley.

ABOVE
At Oakley Farm, a 19th-century manor in northern Virginia, decorator
Katie Ridder and architect Peter Pennoyer designed kitchen cabinets that extend to the
ceiling to take advantage of often-wasted space; a rolling library ladder
provides easy access to out-of-reach shelves.

OPPOSITE
The pristine Connecticut kitchen of
decorator Kristiina Ratia opens
onto a dining area featuring old schoolhouse
chairs painted snow-white; Ratia designed
the custom-made cabinet to stow
her serving pieces and stacks of china.

RIGHT
Fashion designer Cynthia Rowley
stretched theatrical scrim to
screen her open kitchen from the living
area of her Manhattan loft.

BELOW
Mies van der Rohe's Cantilever
chairs and a table by Tucker Robbins
add a sculptural quality to
the Water Mill, New York, kitchen of
Kristina and David Rosenberg,
which was designed in collaboration
with Steven Sclaroff.

PRECEDING PAGES
Real-estate entrepreneur Julie Greenwood mixed
an antique French dining table and cabinet, an Italian chandelier,
and a Viking range in her Fredericksburg, Texas,
kitchen; the original dirt floor has been paved with limestone
gathered on the property.

OPPOSITE
In their Southampton, New York, kitchen,
Coach president and executive creative director Reed Krakoff
and his wife, Delphine, an interior designer, paired
a vintage Saarinen Tulip table with Louis XV dining chairs
upholstered in a custom-made turquoise
ostrich leather from Coach.

ABOVE
Form Architecture + Interiors designed a modernist
kitchen for the Brooklyn loft of clients
Andrew Arrick and Michael Hofemann; the counter is cast
concrete, the sky-blue refrigerator is by
Müller Möbelfabrikation, and the barstools
are from Design Within Reach.

LEFT
The streamlined Hamptons kitchen of tastemaking
couple Peri Wolfman and Charley Gold is
designed for entertaining on a large scale, with two sinks, two
dishwashers, and a commodious center island.

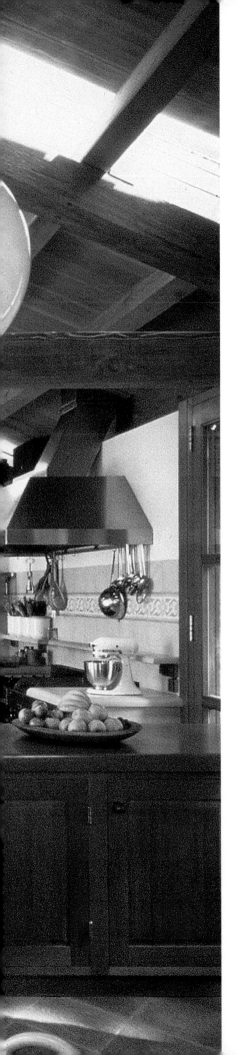

"OUR KITCHEN IS WARM;
IT'S WHO WE ARE. AND IT HAS EVERYTHING.
HONESTLY, I COULD GET RID
OF THE REST OF THE HOUSE AND JUST
LIVE IN THE KITCHEN"
— *Adrian Kahan,*
Ralph Lauren Home executive

LEFT
Inspired by the pared-down Shaker aesthetic,
Italian fashion photographer Oliviero Toscani designed
his kitchen in Tuscany with beautifully crafted
wood cabinetry; the rustic Douglas-fir beams were
salvaged from a warehouse on San Francisco Bay.

ABOVE
Decorator Peter Dunham mixed tawny wood tones
in the Hollywood Hills kitchen of screenwriter
Adam Herz and his wife, Laurie; the upholstered
barstools are a Dunham design.

OPPOSITE
Adrian Kahan, Ralph Lauren Home's vice president of marketing and
communications, and her husband, Bob Leibowitz, added a three-room extension comprising
an eat-in kitchen, larder, and pantry to their Wainscott, New York, retreat;
open shelves display their collection of vintage cookie jars.

ABOVE
In his Hudson Valley weekend home, designer Mark Cunningham painted the
cabinets and walls dove-gray, stained the pine-plank floors, and paired antique benches
with a French zinc-top table.

ABOVE
In the kitchen area of photographer Pieter Estersohn's
Gramercy Park penthouse, 1920s Art Deco chairs
are pulled up to a pair of André Arbus tables; the undercounter
refrigerator is by Sub-Zero, and the vintage
wall cabinet is by Jean Prouvé and Charlotte Perriand.

RIGHT
Lipstick-red kitchen cabinetry by Schiffini
makes a stylish statement in the Manhattan townhouse of
fashion designer Nanette Lepore and her
husband, Robert Savage.

OPPOSITE
The Paris kitchen of Dimonah and Mehmet Iksel—
who create exquisite wall coverings as
Iksel Decorative Arts—features distinctive
wallpaper and fabric from their firm; the open
cabinets are concealed by custom-
made rolling blinds.

OPPOSITE
Lynn Forester de Rothschild's Michael S. Smith–designed
Manhattan kitchen features a double range
by Viking and a custom-made pot rack and barstools.

LEFT
The Paris kitchen of children's-wear designer
Cordelia de Castellane includes a well-planned breakfast area
for her young family; plastic Tam Tam
stools lend a casual vibe to the room's traditional style.

BELOW
Elegant restraint is in evidence at fashion
designer/decorator/author Michael
Leva's Litchfield County, Connecticut, weekend house; vintage
American and Venetian glassware is displayed
in cabinetry by Stephen Piscuskas
of York Street Studio, and the mercury-glass
pendant shades are vintage.

OPPOSITE
Key elements of the Upper East Side
penthouse kitchen of Georgette Farkas, communications
director for chef Daniel Boulud, and
her husband, Peter Trapp, include a Blue Star range,
Best hood, and GE Monogram microwave;
the wall color is Benjamin Moore's Pink Mix, which serves
as a striking foil for the dark-painted cabinets.

ABOVE
The kitchen of chefs Christine and Michel Guérard
in Eugénie-les-Bains, France, was designed
for both business and pleasure; the luxe range and
cabinetry make a grand statement, while the country-style
table and chairs complement the warmth and
intimacy of meals truly savored.

LEFT
In Los Angeles, decorator Kristen Buckingham
created an inviting setting for her
husband, Fleetwood Mac's Lindsey Buckingham, and their
young family; the ovens and range are by Wolf,
the refrigerators are by Sub-Zero, and
the floor is paved in patterned cement tiles.

ABOVE
The Manhattan duplex decorator Ray Booth
shares with MTV Networks marketing
executive John Shea features an open kitchen/dining area
anchored by a 1960s table and a set of
armchairs Booth copied to match a vintage original;
the cabinetry is white oak, and the
backsplash is sheathed in glass-mosaic
tile by Waterworks.

RIGHT
Architect Sig Bergamin devised a tidy
breakfast area in the kitchen of his New York City
pied-à-terre with a hinged table that drops
to the wall and folding chairs.

OPPOSITE
In the Hollywood Hills, designers
Robin Standefer and Stephen Alesch of Roman
and Williams created an up-to-date
kitchen with an old-world
feel for actors Ben Stiller and
Christine Taylor.

"KITCHENS SHOULD BE DESIGNED
AROUND WHAT'S TRULY IMPORTANT—FUN,
FOOD, AND LIFE"

— *Daniel Boulud, chef/restaurateur*

ABOVE
In San Miguel de Allende, Mexico, whitewashed
pine cabinetry and bold Talavera tiles add
warmth to a kitchen decorated by
Anne-Marie Midy and Jorge Almada.

RIGHT
Milk-glass light fixtures are suspended over vintage
chairs and a stone-top table in the Manhattan
townhouse of decorator Steven Gambrel and Chris
Connor; the double sink was custom made,
and the limestone floor is by Exquisite Surfaces.

ABOVE
Folding garden chairs surround
actor Pierre Arditi's Directoire table in the
kitchen of his Normandy farmhouse;
the backsplash is paved in antique tile.

RIGHT
Blue-and-white tiles are
used to striking effect in a 17th-century
kitchen in Mexico.

OPPOSITE
In the weekend cottage
of decorators William Yeoward and
Colin Orchard in rural England,
Yeoward commissioned a hand-painted wall
treatment to mimic the look of
red-and-white gingham; the
kitchen cupboard displays cheerful
ironstone china.

STYLE GUIDE

▪ When you start a kitchen redo, be sure you know what you own: Make a list of your equipment, from copper pots to standing mixers, before you decide on cabinets. It's better to have too much storage than too little; that goes for counter space too.

▪ If you often cook for a crowd and use large pans, opt for deep, generous sinks without compartments. Even better, have two—a prep sink and a troughlike version for washing pots and dishes. And a pair of dishwashers, one for glassware, another for plates, means nothing is ever left to clean the next day.

▪ The best kitchens have drawers for everything, from frying pans and utensils to spices and cereal; drawers keep counters clutter-free.

▪ A pantry sounds like an old-fashioned luxury, but once you've had one—whether a madeover closet or a separate area designed for everything from tableware to canned goods to small appliances—your culinary life will never be the same.

▪ Surfaces create the look and style of a kitchen: Cabinets, counters, walls, and floors offer the chance to choose simple and classic or to go for a more distinctive look. In particular, backsplashes are a terrific blank canvas that can be sheathed in sleek tilework, inlaid mosaics, antiqued mirror, or barn wood without a big commitment or investment.

▪ Forewarned is forearmed, so research the stain-repelling qualities of every material that appeals to you, whether for counters or floors. Given the probable wear and tear in your kitchen's future—spills, scratches, and more—you need to know what will stay relatively pristine and what will still look great with a bit of patina.

▪ If you are a neatnik, a glass-doored refrigerator-cum–display case might be just your thing. If its contents are likely to be a bit of a jumble, however, a standard solid door is a better choice.

▪ Think quick fix if you find your budget less substantial than your wish list: Painting cabinets, updating hardware, and installing an inexpensive new floor can transform your kitchen in a weekend.

LEFT
Stacks of china and earthenware—vintage and contemporary—line the kitchen shelves of decorator/author Tricia Foley's Yaphank, New York, home; the range is by Thermador, and a repurposed aquarium stand serves as an island.

PRIVATE SPACES

BEDROOMS & BOUDOIRS

BATHS

CHILDREN'S ROOMS

BEDROOMS & BOUDOIRS

No space in a home serves as a refuge more than a bedroom. Shut its door and the irritations of the nine-to-five life should recede and the clamor of the outside world become muffled and distant. Privacy is key, comfort is paramount, and orderliness is crucial, whether it is an elegant multiroom master suite tailored to your needs or a spare room designed with the care and cosseting of overnight guests in mind. In *Billy Baldwin Decorates,* the designer observes, "The bedroom ought to be the most personal room in the house. Everything should contribute to an atmosphere of peace. For some, this means extreme neatness—just the necessities, with plenty of space between. Others make their bedrooms part sitting room and invite friends there for tea or drinks." Certain prerequisites always apply, whatever square footage is under consideration: a top-quality mattress, a bedside table or two—preferably large enough to hold books, a lamp, a pretty vase of flowers, and a clock—plus storage for clothing. But designing a bedroom to be a retreat where you can relax and recharge doesn't mean settling for subdued and unsexy, so stamp it with your singular taste—or the combined tastes of you and your loved one. Employ its walls as a gallery for your collections, from soothing landscapes to jazzy abstract works of art, and for those with a vanity or dressing table, keep your accessories arranged with panache. If your style is formal, grace the room with a canopy that rises to the ceiling with aristocratic pomp; if your preferences are more restrained, a Zenlike sleeping platform hugging the floor might please. Choose a palette as colorless as a spring cloud, or lavish the walls with a pattern so dramatic—like an overscale ikat—that the room requires few if any ornaments. And if you are lucky enough to have a walk-in closet or dressing room, you have not only the means to keep your clothing tidy and easily accessible, you have a private place to express your personal flair with utter self-indulgence. ■

PRECEDING PAGES
Interior designer Vicente Wolf used an abundance of
Manuel Canovas's Soliman fabric to create
a serene boudoir for a client in
Manhattan's Museum Tower; a Donghia table and
chairs flank the luxe canopied daybed.

OPPOSITE
Scores of British royal portraits keep
watch over Paul Donaher's master bedroom in Water Mill,
New York, which was decorated in collaboration
with his designer friend Nannette Brown;
the 18th-century ebonized bed was found at the
Brimfield antiques fair in Massachusetts.

ABOVE
At Hobble Diamond Ranch, the Montana
vacation home of Susan and Robert Burch, London-based
decorators Philip Hooper and Sally Metcalfe
added a bucolic touch to the master bedroom with a birch
four-poster by Diane Cole Ross.

RIGHT
Magazine editor Dara Caponigro rigged filmy
mosquito netting as a romantic canopy in the master bedroom
of the Hudson Valley lakefront house she
shares with her young family.

OPPOSITE
The Germantown, New York, bedroom
of interior designer Gaser
Tabakoglu, a protégé of Renzo Mongiardino,
features awning stripes and
a dramatic tomato-red four-poster.

ABOVE
In Malibu, California, Cindy Crawford and
Rande Gerber's master bedroom, designed by
Michael S. Smith, opens onto a
terrace overlooking the sea; the bed linens
are by Nancy Koltes, and the mid-20th-century rugs
by the Beni Ouarain tribe are
from Brooke Pickering Moroccan Rugs.

LEFT
Floor-to-ceiling windows in former
dancer Rita Noroña Schrager's master bedroom—
located in one of Richard Meier's
dramatic glass towers on Manhattan's West Side
and decorated by Gabriel de la Portilla—
are hidden behind Margot silk
curtains by the Silk Trading Co.; the bed
is Anglo-Indian.

ABOVE
Artist Frank Faulkner painted the
mantel and ceiling of his Hudson, New York, guest
room pure white to highlight
its espresso-brown walls; the bedcover
is made from antique toile de Jouy,
and the painted screen
is from Niall Smith Antiques.

RIGHT
In his 1740s Dutch Colonial in New
York's Hudson Valley, designer Mark Cunningham
tacked a linen panel to the wall as
a headboard; the bedding is by Ralph Lauren
Home, and the Hudson's Bay
blanket is by Woolrich.

OPPOSITE
Decorator Matthew Patrick Smyth
installed an 18th-century Moghul façade
from a merchant's house as a
headboard in the master bedroom of a documentary-
filmmaker client in London; the
hand-blocked fabrics are from India, and
the suzani is 19th century.

PRECEDING PAGES
The astute eye of fashion designer Bill Blass is reflected in the refined
master bedroom of his 1770s Connecticut country
house; the staircase model is from H. M. Luther, an antique American quilt
covers the bed, and crisp white moldings set off the
chocolate-brown walls.

LEFT
Château de Jonquay, the Normandy summer home of
Amy and Todd Hase, cofounders of Todd Hase Furniture, features a tower
bedroom papered in Simply Stripes
by Brunschwig & Fils; the daybed is 19th-century French.

ABOVE
Modern-furniture guru Troy Halterman displays blue-chip
photography salon style in the master bedroom of his Fifth Avenue
apartment; the walls are painted
black, and the Arne Jacobsen Egg chair is vintage.

OPPOSITE
In a bedroom at Villa Le Rose, Leonardo and Maria Beatrice Ferragamo's 15th-century house outside Florence, the chinoiserie details were inspired by the frescoes on the walls; the pagoda canopy is fashioned from the same silk as the curtains.

RIGHT
The idiosyncratic flavor of an artist's studio is evoked by the Manhattan penthouse of fashion designer Ralph Rucci; the panel of reproduction 18th-century wallpaper is by Gracie, the Louis XV stool is outfitted in crocodile, and the bed linens are by Frette.

BELOW
Antiques dealer Alexandre Biaggi used a lyrical Boussac cotton for the walls, headboard, and curtains of his Paris bedroom; a Serge Matta India-ink sketch for a Schiaparelli scarf is displayed above the bed.

OPPOSITE
Spring-green toile wallpaper and fabric
set a cheerful tone at decorator Anne Coyle's Chicago
apartment; the marble-top gueridon is
from Ballard Designs, and the 1940s chandelier
is from Pavilion Antiques.

ABOVE
In the nap room of the East Hampton,
New York, weekend house she shares with her husband,
Barry Friedberg, interior designer Charlotte Moss
layered a bevy of floral prints to create
a summery air.

LEFT
Art consultant Quito Fierro sheathed
the walls of his Paris guest room in a Pierre Frey
stripe; the bed is from Lieux,
and the 1950s French chairs are from
Maroun H. Saloum.

TOP LEFT
Decorator Muriel Brandolini placed an intricate wrought-iron
bed in the media/guest room of her Manhattan
townhouse; the artwork is by Donald Baechler, and
Brandolini's collage of straw papers
and grass cloth was applied to the walls by Cameron Prather.

CENTER LEFT
The walls of the master bedroom of a Midwestern Victorian
decorated by Patrick Naggar and Terese Carpenter
of Nile are stenciled with a golden frieze; the circa-1880 Aesthetic
Movement furniture is by Pottier & Stymus.

ABOVE
In a bedroom in their Paris home,
Lorraine and Patrick Frey of Pierre Frey backed
the headboard with a wall of bookshelves; the Coutances
toile linens are by Pierre Frey for Yves Delorme.

LEFT
The Philadelphia guest room of Anthropologie president
Glen Senk and the firm's antiques buyer, Keith
Johnson, features an 18th-century peasant wedding bed
and a collection of framed antique toile fabrics.

OPPOSITE
A cotton-gauze print by Robert Kime from John Rosselli
curtains a guest-room bed at architect
Gil Schafer's weekend house in Amenia, New York.

OPPOSITE
The walls of a small guest room in
the New York City townhouse of Chris Connor
and designer Steven Gambrel
are covered in a vintage Uzbek ikat; the
custom-made bed linens are
by Casa Del Bianco.

ABOVE
In the Brentwood, California, master
bedroom of designer Michael S. Smith, a chaise
longue by T. H. Robsjohn-Gibbings,
bedding by Calvin Klein Home,
and a vintage suzani.

LEFT
At La Zahia, the Marrakech
retreat of couturier Yves Saint Laurent
and partner Pierre Bergé, a guest-
room's tester bed is sheathed in lipstick-
red fabric.

159

"REAL COMFORT,
VISUAL AND PHYSICAL, IS VITAL
TO EVERY ROOM"

— *Mark Hampton, decorator*

LEFT
The bed in interior designer Jamie Drake's taxicab-yellow
Manhattan bedroom is upholstered in a Clarence
House zebra-print silk; lacquer bedside tables, custom-made
bed linens by E. Braun & Co., and a pair of Gene Davis
silkscreens showcase Drake's flair for drama.

ABOVE
In the downtown New York master bedroom of
fashion and accessories designers Ranjana and Naeem Khan,
a mirror wall sculpture serves as a headboard and reflects
a 1960s starburst chandelier; the coverlet and pillows were
custom made by Naeem Khan Home.

ABOVE
A bedroom at the Bedford, New York,
estate of decorators Stephen Sills
and James Huniford of Stephen Sills Associates
is painted glossy olive-green; next
to the Italian Empire steel bed is a Louis XVI
child's chair covered in horsehair.

LEFT
Silk curtains soften the lines
of the wood canopy bed in the Paris
pied-à-terre of Mario Grauso,
president of the fashion
division of the luxury group Puig, and
his wife, Anne.

OPPOSITE
Views of North America wallpaper by
Zuber sheathes Elizabeth and
David Netto's Greenwich Village bedroom;
the Louis XVI–style chair is from the
estate of tastemaker Carlos de Beistegui.

OPPOSITE
In the center of his New York City
loft bedroom, decorator
Vicente Wolf floated an upholstered bed
of his own design on the diagonal.

RIGHT
At a Venezuelan retreat designed by
architect Fernando Arriaga, a
guest room opens to a dramatic view; the
space is furnished with a concrete
bed and an African chair, and the floor
is sandblasted marble.

BELOW
Master curtainmaker Monte Coleman
fashioned a tailored sleeping alcove
in his pint-size Manhattan studio, topping a
built-in platform with a custom-made
Charles H. Beckley mattress.

ABOVE
In London, an 18th-century Ottoman tapestry is the focal point of Jimmy Choo founder Tamara Mellon's bedroom, decorated by Martyn Lawrence-Bullard; the bed skirt and pillows are made of a custom-embroidered fabric by the Silk Trading Co., and 1960s mercury-glass lamps are set atop '40s French bedside chests.

RIGHT
Fashion designer Zang Toi refinished the antique mahogany bed in his Manhattan bedroom with layers of glossy black paint and silver-plated its golden ormolu trim; the 19th-century chandelier is ornamented with silver-plate instruments.

OPPOSITE
The centerpiece of decorator Bunny Williams's Park Avenue bedroom is an extraordinary Serge Roche–style mirrored bed; she upholstered its headboard in a fanciful embroidered silk from India.

OPPOSITE
Pastel cottons and silk veils bring
romance to the Jade Room at nightclub impresario
Jaouad Kadiri's Marrakech home; the
Venetian-style mirror was made by craftsmen in Tangier.

ABOVE
Antiques dealer Patrick Timewell layered floral
patterns in his Moroccan bedroom;
Indian-cotton panels were hung to dress the walls.

LEFT
Decorator Miles Redd used De Gournay's
Earlham chinoiserie wall covering for the Manhattan
bedroom of writer Shyama Patel, who is
shown wearing a hand-embroidered skirt from New Delhi;
the black-lacquer cabinets are
vintage Chinese, and the sconces are Bill Blass
designs for Visual Comfort.

ABOVE
A 1920s Venetian chandelier adds color and
spirit to the Brooklyn bedroom of
Stéphane and Frouwkje Pagani of the lighting firm
PaganiStudio; the Belgian-linen curtains
are from Pottery Barn.

RIGHT
Photographer Kelly Klein's Wellington,
Florida, getaway features a bed custom made by
Calvin Klein Home dressed with the
firm's bedding; the floor is covered with Japanese
tatami matting.

OPPOSITE
At decorator Tom Scheerer's retreat in
Harbour Island, Bahamas, the master bedroom—
which was formerly a chapel—is
dominated by a massive stainless-steel
four-poster.

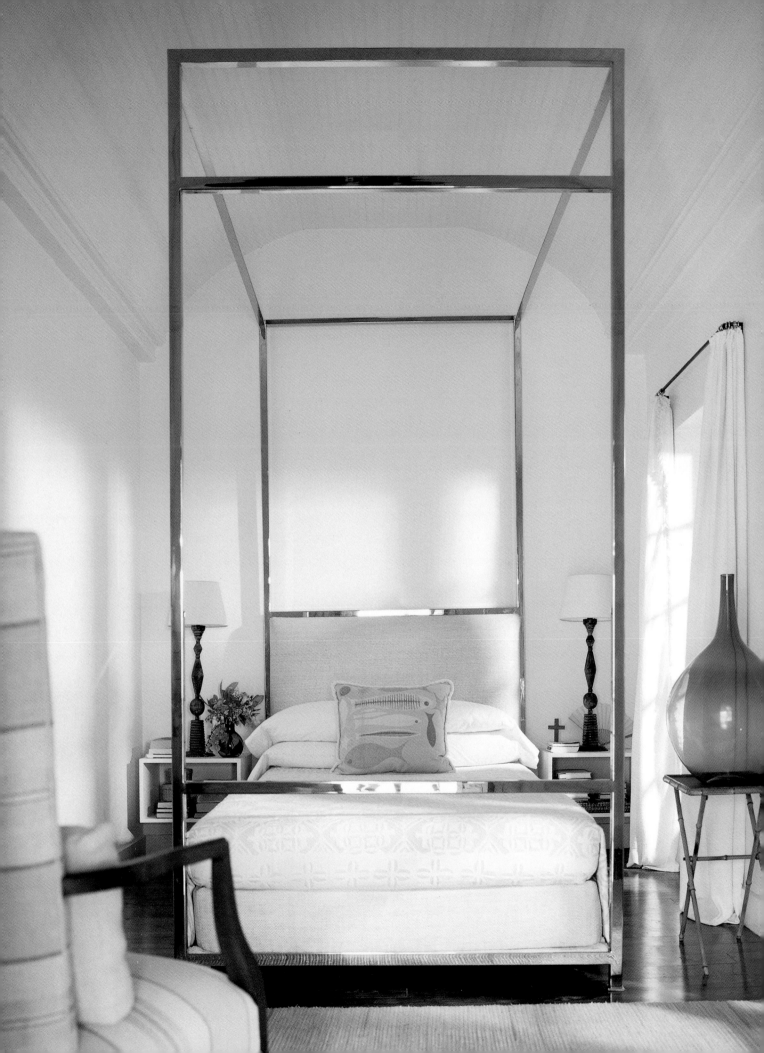

ABOVE
The ethereal guest room at Eugenie Voorhees's
Hugh Newell Jacobsen—designed Nantucket house features
wall-mounted bedside drawers by Jacobsen
and a floor painted glossy white.

RIGHT
In her Manhattan penthouse duplex, designed in collaboration
with Jay Smith and Chris Howard, fashion stylist
Barbara Dente installed a sculptural white marble staircase
that descends into a serenely spartan bedroom.

"MY BED IS
THE PLACE I FEEL
THE MOST
RELAXED AND THE MOST
SECURE.
AND CERTAINLY
THE MOST
RESTED"

— *Vera Wang, fashion designer*

STYLE GUIDE

▪ Nearly everyone has a memory of the perfect hotel room, one where you felt free, easy, and pampered—so keep that reverie in mind as you plan your bedroom. What details made that particular space a four-star experience? Try working many of them into your own retreat; even without room service, your place can be just as luxurious.

▪ Canopies are glamorous and theatrical. If the idea of sleeping in a curtained bed appeals to you, go for it; you can even mimic the look by installing narrow ceiling rods above your bed and hanging fabric panels. And why not change the look with the season? Rich silk damask, velvet, and wool challis give coziness to a chilly winter room, while gauzy linen, embroidered cotton voile, and even mosquito netting are ideal for the summer months or a warm-weather locale.

▪ Bedside tables should be generous, big enough for a lamp, books, and everything you need close at hand. If you prefer a clutter-free sleeping area, install sconces or swing-arm lamps to flank your bed and select bedside cabinets with ample storage. Those with a narrow pullout shelf are handy for a nighttime water carafe or a book.

▪ If your bed frame doesn't accommodate a bed skirt and has an exposed box spring, mask it with a mattress pad and fitted sheet or have a cover made for a more pulled-together look.

▪ Invest in the best mattress you can afford, even if it means cutting corners in another area of your bedroom-decorating budget. Take time to test it in the store before you commit, and once it's delivered, use a down-filled mattress cover to provide extra softness under your bed linens.

LEFT
In jewelry designer Fruzsina Keehn's London bedroom, decorated in collaboration with Alex Papachristidis, are a pair of 19th-century French gilt-wood mirrors and an antique German commode; the curtains are dove-gray silk taffeta.

OPPOSITE
The San Francisco dressing room of designers
Jeffry Weisman and Andrew Fisher
of Fisher Weisman features a pair of Mies van der Rohe's
Barcelona stools by Knoll and shutters made
from antique Indian screens.

ABOVE
Dudley, a pug belonging to
Los Angeles–based decorator Natasha Esch,
occupies a drawer in the
Chinese-silk-lined Victorian armoire
Esch uses as a shoe closet.

TOP RIGHT
At a Caribbean villa designed by
Philip Hooper of Sibyl Colefax & John Fowler,
the dressing room is kitted
out with limed-teak cabinets inlaid
with mother-of-pearl.

RIGHT
Decorator Steven Gambrel crafted
a bespoke dressing area for a Manhattan client
with ebonized shelving
trimmed with square brass tacks.

ABOVE
The spacious master bathroom of the Bel Air,
California, home interior designer Michael S. Smith shares
with James Costos does double duty
as a dressing area with glass-front closets; the Town
tub and fittings are by Smith for Kallista.

TOP RIGHT
At the Upper West Side apartment of Calvin Tsao
and Zack McKown of Tsao & McKown Architects, neckties
are draped over wall-mounted towel hooks
in the customized dressing room.

CENTER RIGHT
Floor-to-ceiling shelves harbor hundreds of
T-shirts in columnist Billy Norwich's New York City closet,
which is cleverly concealed behind a wall of
faux books in his bedroom.

RIGHT
Decorator J. Randall Powers designed a combination
dressing room/bath for the Houston home
he shares with Bill Caudell; their luggage is stowed
on open shelves for easy access.

OPPOSITE
Joe Nahem and Tom Fox of Fox-Nahem Design
created a sybaritic dressing room in the
Manhattan duplex of Luigi Caiola and Sean McGill; the
cabinetry is of cerused oak, the lantern
is of Murano glass, and the writing desk is
vintage André Sornay.

STYLE GUIDE

■ If the indulgence of a walk-in dressing area isn't in your budget, don't despair: Pint-size closets can be decorated too. Paint their walls a kicky color or line them in a pretty wallpaper that complements the color scheme of your bedroom or bath.

■ Plan your closets carefully to ensure your clothing is properly and safely stored. For example, any items kept on hangers should have enough space to be hung without wrinkling or getting snagged.

■ Fabric-covered hangers are best (those sheathed in velvet prevent straps from slipping off), followed by the traditional wood variety. There's nothing so chic as rows of perfectly matched hangers—for everything from dresses and blouses to suits and slacks. Purchase them by the case; it's a small investment that adds a luxe, made-to-order look.

■ Organize shoes by stowing pairs in individual plastic boxes (they can be bought in bulk online) with a photo of the shoes inside facing out; those less ambitious can use a labelmaker to identify the contents. Think of this as a visual filing system—and an ideal project for a rainy afternoon.

■ Stuff the toes of your shoes with fabric-covered cotton pads or tissue paper between wearings; wood trees will keep men's shoes in shape.

■ To better organize your jewelry, buy velvet-lined trays that can be stacked on shelves or tucked in drawers; they will make it easier to keep earrings in pairs and necklaces untangled.

OPPOSITE
High style reigns in the Manhattan dressing room of fashion designer Nanette Lepore; her toy poodle, Bunny, perches on a custom-made ottoman. The Chinese Art Deco rug is from ABC Carpet & Home.

TOP RIGHT
There are more than 400 pairs of Jimmy Choos lined up in company founder Tamara Mellon's London closet; the embroidered table cover was found in Marrakech.

CENTER RIGHT
Decorator Renzo Mongiardino upholstered a hall of closets at Villa Vistorta, the Brandolini-family estate in Italy's Veneto region, in green felt accented with yellow braid; the opaline-glass urn is early-19th-century French.

RIGHT
Fashion designer Anna Sui purchased a penthouse several floors above her New York City apartment to use as an entertaining space/retreat/dressing area; her treasure trove of clothing and accessories is displayed in its walk-in closet.

BATHS

With all the moisture and daily use bathrooms face, you'll probably need to remodel yours at least once, so make the most of the opportunity and transform your bath into a space that both relaxes and delights you. In addition to sculptural tubs, artful light fixtures, paneling, stone, and exotic wall coverings, many homeowners are now getting on board with eco-friendly options like water-saving faucets and tanks that recycle gray water for the garden. Think architecturally too, whether you are planning to add a bath or renovate: They can be tucked under eaves for coziness or opened up with a glass wall that takes in treetops and clear blue skies. Tile choices are endless, from delft to Deco, from great glazed squares to intricate micromosaics. And while many people's bath ideal is the pared-down luxe of an ultramodern spa or a hammam, British decorator David Hicks liked to emphasize the "room" aspect of the word *bathroom,* noting that these utilitarian areas can "benefit greatly from atmosphere, and this can be achieved by using pattern, pictures, good lighting, interesting color, and wallpaper." Consider furnishing the bath as fully and as fashionably as you would any other room in the house. Place a table alongside the tub for flowers, a scented candle, and a book; install narrow shelves all around for the display of photos or a collection of perfume bottles; or sheathe the space in a lyrical wall covering. Box in a freestanding footed tub to make it more sophisticated, encasing its curves in sleek marble or a handsome wood surround. If you have a particularly large room, bring in a dressing table, bookcase, or armoire—or a cotton-terry-covered chair or settee to perch on while you take off your shoes or for a talkative spouse to keep you company as you lather up. The important thing is to combine visual charm and physical comfort into a powerful representation of your personality. ∎

PRECEDING PAGES
For a guest bath at a client's Montecito, California,
estate, decorator Michael S. Smith
commissioned reproductions of antique tiles he found in
Portugal; Vaughan sconces flank the mirror.

ABOVE
Architect Hugh Newell Jacobsen designed a
hammered-copper bathtub for Kate and Jim Lehrer's 18th-century
West Virginia house; a trio of banker's-style wall
lamps provides soft light.

RIGHT
On the Greek island of Patmos, artist Holly Lueders
installed a marble sink below a
charming frescoed backsplash in her master bath.

OPPOSITE
At Mila and Tom Tuttle's Greek Revival
townhouse in Manhattan, decorator Miles Redd used
De Gournay's Early Views of India wallpaper
in the master bath; the undermount sinks are by Kohler.

"I DON'T KNOW IF LESS IS MORE OR MORE IS LESS"

— *David Gill, gallerist*

OPPOSITE
Jean-Pascal Lévy-Trumet, a French stage designer
and director, created a futuristic master
bath at his Paris house; it is outfitted with
sheet-metal paneling, a custom-made
egg-shaped concrete tub, and a 1950s light fixture.

ABOVE
The master bath of interior designers George
Yabu and Glenn Pushelberg of Yabu Pushelberg,
which overlooks a ravine and forest behind
their Toronto home, evokes the feeling of a tree
house; the Spoon tub is by G. P. Benedini for Agape.

TOP LEFT
Decorator Katie Ridder chose a
Queen Anne—style mirror
and glossy green paint for a powder room in
Carol and Shelby Bonnie's San Francisco home, then
studded the walls with playful
painted-aluminum flowers.

ABOVE
In former dancer Shelley Washington's
Greenwich Village penthouse, designer Vicente Wolf
encircled a claw-foot tub with a plastic
shower curtain he customized with black
grosgrain ribbon.

LEFT
The graphic pattern of Clarence House's Large
Stripe wallpaper was hung horizontally
by architect Steven Learner in the guest bath at his
family's downtown Manhattan loft.

OPPOSITE
In Paris, Jamie Creel and Marco Scarani
painted stripes down the walls and across the ceiling
of their master bath; the nickel-and-brass
tub is 19th century, and the Honoré Paris chair is from
Galerie Yves Gastou.

OPPOSITE
An Ellsworth Kelly drawing
adds a grace note to
the minimalist bath of photographer Kelly
Klein in Wellington, Florida;
the Spoon tub is by Agape.

ABOVE
Cedar paneling sheathes the walls
and tub surround in a
bath at architect Alan Wanzenberg's
bayside house in Water Island, New York,
lending the space a warm,
organic flavor.

LEFT
In Montauk, New York, decorator
Vicente Wolf's master
bath opens onto a private deck with an
outdoor shower; the copper tub
is antique.

OPPOSITE
A frosted-glass wall separating
the library and the master
bath in designer Vicente Wolf's Manhattan
loft allows sunlight into the room-size
limestone shower;
the fittings are by Waterworks.

LEFT
Wolf installed a brushed-steel
sink basin atop an
antique table in the adjoining dressing
area; Ron Arad's plastic T. Vac
chair is by Vitra.

BELOW
The marble-clad North Sea, New York,
master bath of architect
Lee F. Mindel faces a waterside bird
sanctuary; the tub is by Kohler, the .25 bath
and shower fittings are by Shelton,
Mindel & Associates for Waterworks,
and the floor is quartzite.

TOP LEFT
Decorator Eric Hughes deployed
matching sinks in the master bath of actor Hank Azaria's
Manhattan loft; vintage apothecary bottles
are displayed on glass shelves.

BELOW
A client's Malibu, California, weekend house gets a seaside makeover
courtesy of interior designer Kerry Joyce, who lined the room
with shallow shelving to display starfish and shells;
the walls are painted a pale aqua by Donald Kaufman Color.

CENTER LEFT
In the Southampton, New York, cottage of
designer Muriel Brandolini, a tranquil bath features a cotton-veiled
footed tub and a floor painted robin's-egg-blue.

BOTTOM LEFT
In a bath at art-and-antiques dealer Pierre
Passebon's retreat in rural France, decorator Jacques Grange
referenced the work of Swedish designer
Carl Larsson by utilizing narrow strips of molding to add
detail to the white-lacquered walls.

OPPOSITE
At Lime Close, garden designer Marie-Christine
de Laubarède's manor in the English countryside, a guest
bath is nestled under the eaves.

OPPOSITE
The Bahia, Brazil, getaway of
longtime Valentino public-relations
consultant Charlene de Ganay
is a seductive retreat, with a polished-cement
sunken tub and open shower in
the center of a sprawling master bath.

ABOVE
In Sag Harbor, New York, the Annabelle
Selldorf–designed weekend home of hairstylist
Kevin Mancuso juxtaposes the sleek
surfaces of a minimalist bath with an adjacent
slatted-wood outdoor-shower deck.

LEFT
Photographer Anita Calero carved space
for a narrow bathroom with a porthole
window in her Manhattan loft; the wall-mounted
sink is oak, and the Tara fittings
are by Dornbracht.

ABOVE
Understated glamour is the theme of the Bel Air, California,
bathroom of fashion designer Monique Lhuillier, which includes
a deep built-in tub, white-oak cabinetry, wall-to-wall
mirror, and a custom-made glittery light fixture; the photograph,
Divers, is an iconic 1930 image by
fashion photographer George Hoyningen-Huene.

RIGHT
Designers Robin Standefer and Stephen Alesch of
Roman and Williams conjured a sense of
Art Deco elegance in the Hollywood Hills bath of actors Christine Taylor
and Ben Stiller. Paved floor-to-ceiling with subway tile limned
in marine-blue, the room features sconces and
an antique medical cabinet from Urban Archaeology;
the tub is by the Water Monopoly.

OPPOSITE
At the Marrakech retreat of Yves Saint Laurent
and Pierre Bergé, designer Bill Willis
created a sublime, sophisticated setting using
an intricate interplay of green
and black marble with turquoise mosaics.

ABOVE
Decorator Muriel Brandolini's
hand-blocked fabrics dress the walls and
ceiling of her Upper East Side
master bath; the shell chandelier is
by Claire Cormier-Fauvel.

LEFT
The Carrara-marble-sheathed
bath in fashion designer Giambattista Valli's
Rome apartment is filled with
exotic treasures, including an elephant
statue from Jaipur and a
Japanese bonsai-tree sculpture.

OPPOSITE
A humdrum prewar bathroom—with vintage fixtures and a checkerboard-tile floor—
in the uptown Manhattan apartment shared by Polo Ralph Lauren
executives Tom Bezucha and Margaret "Sam" Hamilton received a fast, fashion-forward makeover via a cheery
striped shower curtain by Ralph Lauren Home and a charming antique side chair.

ABOVE
In the cozy bath of the Martha's Vineyard cottage that serves as a
seaside retreat for Corky and Stephen Pollan and their family, classic porcelain fixtures
and painted paneling present a low-key elegance.

TOP LEFT
Pages taken from *Cabinet of Natural Curiosities*
by Albertus Seba line the powder room
walls at the Sag Harbor, New York, home of Chris Connor
and decorator Steven Gambrel.

CENTER LEFT
An open shower/bathing area in the
master bath of the downtown Manhattan loft of
architect Steven Learner and his
family is sheathed in gleaming cobalt subway tile.

ABOVE
In the master bath of her West Village loft,
model/artist Anh Duong is seated at
her dressing table; Julian Schnabel's painting *Anh* is
displayed on the right-hand wall.

LEFT AND OPPOSITE
Each of the six brilliantly tiled
bathrooms at Dar Es Saada—the guesthouse at
couturier Yves Saint Laurent's Marrakech
retreat—was designed by Bill
Willis in a different and distinctive style.

STYLE GUIDE

■ Bath fixtures, faucets, and hardware represent a sizable investment, so be sure to choose carefully. When in doubt, always opt for a more streamlined style and classic finish, be it contemporary or retro. The same guidelines apply to surface materials, from paint and wallpaper to tile and stone: If you're concerned about resale value, go for elegant over edgy, and your bath will never look dated.

■ Easy-care surfaces are key, especially if you have children, so think twice about showers and baths with sleek glass walls or doors; they look terrific but tend to spot unless squeegeed after use.

■ Simplify your life by stacking fresh towels on open shelves under your sink or on a nearby étagère; fold them straight from the dryer, stow promptly, and never rummage through a linen closet again.

■ Medicine cabinets can now come equipped with an outlet to plug in your hair dryer or toothbrush; some even have an inset TV or a mini refrigerator. If you like bells and whistles, the latest technology guarantees there are plenty to choose from.

■ Analyze your bathroom for every possible storage opportunity. If the spacing of the studs allows, why not knock out a section of drywall and make a floor-to-ceiling niche with doors and shallow shelves to hold toiletries and cosmetics?

■ Because of its small square footage, a powder room is the perfect location for a glamorous design gesture. A hand-painted sink basin, over-the-top wall covering, or dazzling chandelier will make your room distinctive. But if you want sexy, moody lighting, don't rely on low-wattage bulbs—install a dimmer. Nose-powdering requires decent light.

LEFT
Interior designer Thomas O'Brien
outfitted the master bath of a client's New York City
apartment with a sink, shower, and
bath fittings from his line for Waterworks;
the double-sink vanity is by his
firm Aero Studios, and the floor is paved in
mosaic tile by Walker Zanger.

CHILDREN'S ROOMS

It's never too early to introduce your son or daughter to the allure of a beautiful room—especially a space that has been designed not only for fun and games but with their education in mind. "In training a child's taste," pioneering American decorator Ruby Ross Wood advised in 1925, "appeal should always be made through the natural inclinations of that child." In other words, pay close attention to the subjects, colors, and fantasies capturing your offspring's imagination, and give them rooms whose decoration has been driven by their creativity and refined by your own sense of style. If fashion is your daughter's obsession, why not frame elegant dress-design sketches or theater illustrations for her room? A whimsical headboard covered in an exotic pattern might reference your son's interest in far-flung lands, just as a wall papered floor to ceiling with nautical charts or overscale maps could be used to teach geography. And any image—from a favorite book cover to artful photos of animals—can now be blown up to create a unique wallpaper to use as an accent or to sheathe an entire room. Myriads of young girls proclaim their preference for pink, but there's no reason a rosy palette has to be teeth-achingly sweet. Try a sophisticated shade of fuchsia, or temper her pick with soft white and touches of lavender, charming paisley fabrics, or a grand work of art that lifts her princess point of view into a scheme that's a bit more chic. Have a professional artist brush a mural onto a wall or personalize a piece of furniture. Customize a bath with brightly colored tiles for the floor and walls, install fanciful wallpaper, or have the tub encased in a painted-wood surround that resembles a magical castle or handsome rowboat. Buy a Palm Beach Moderne pagoda-roofed cabinet, paint it a brilliant color, and place it alongside a bed to hold dolls and books. You could also commission your child to make his own works of art. Just provide the materials, then frame the drawings, paintings, and collages that result. Above all, keep in mind that when it comes to design, it doesn't take much to inspire creativity and to help your children exercise good and bad decisionmaking. Don't forget, we all learn by doing, and experience builds confidence. ■

PRECEDING PAGES
At home in Los Angeles, Georgia Panitch, the daughter of decorator Kristen Panitch and her husband, Sanford, reads inside a cozy curtained bedroom nook created by her mother; the whimsical painting is by Georgia's grandmother Patricia Newman.

TOP LEFT
Elio Estersohn, at ease in his Gramercy Park bedroom; the wall covering is made from a photograph his father, lensman Pieter Estersohn, took in India. The Loft crib is by NettoCollection.

BOTTOM LEFT
At a client's weekend house in Malibu, California, interior designer Kerry Joyce installed a lemon-yellow footed tub and a no-nonsense mosaic-tile directive in a children's bathroom.

BELOW
Jewelry designer Temple St. Clair Carr and her husband, Paul Engler, painted a wall in the children's bath of their New York City townhouse Hermès-orange and installed an industrial-style sink.

OPPOSITE
In Manhattan's West Village, actor Julianne Moore and her husband, writer-director Bart Freundlich, papered the room of their son, Caleb, with a wall-size world map by Hammacher Schlemmer; the cabinet is vintage George Nelson.

BOYS

TOP LEFT
Architect Shamir Shah commissioned
a fanciful mural by Malcolm Hill
in Wainscott, New York, for the three sons
of clients Julie and Bruce Menin;
the playroom features cabinets by Blu Dot
and carpet tiles by Flor.

ABOVE
Philip Hooper of Sibyl Colefax and
John Fowler created a playful teak-and-fiberglass
tub surround in the shape
of a rowboat for a children's bath
at a client's Caribbean retreat.

LEFT
In the Martyn Lawrence-Bullard–decorated
London bedroom of Jimmy Choo
founder Tamara Mellon's daughter, Araminta,
an Uzbek suzani is displayed above a
bed by Pottery Barn Kids.

OPPOSITE
A vintage Jean Royère sconce and fashion sketches
by Bill Blass bring sophistication
to the Manhattan bedroom of Sophie Krakoff, a
daughter of Coach president and
executive creative director Reed Krakoff;
the ottomans are upholstered in Coach suedes.

OPPOSITE
Violet Savage, daughter of fashion designer Nanette Lepore and her husband, Robert Savage, strikes a pose in her West Village bedroom, where a Hunt Slonem canvas is displayed above a custom-made tufted daybed.

ABOVE
The Upper East Side bedroom of Brando Brandolini, son of decorator Muriel Brandolini and her husband, Nuno, features a desk of perforated Corian by Martin Szekely and walls and valances covered in fabrics of Muriel's design.

TOP RIGHT
In Westchester County, New York, interior designer Katie Ridder and her husband, architect Peter Pennoyer, created an exotic retreat for their daughter Gigi with an embroidered headboard by Lisa Fine and bedding by Leontine Linens.

CENTER RIGHT
Decorator Jamie Drake crafted a colorful bookshelf for a children's bedroom in the Manhattan apartment of clients Eleanor and Bobby Cayre; graphic pillows continue the space's sense of playfulness.

RIGHT
Great fun is guaranteed at the New York City townhouse of Lauren Schor and her young family with a bunk-bed puppet theater designed by son Harrison, assisted by design team Wayne Nathan and Carol Egan of Nathan Egan Interiors. Harrison is pictured with siblings Mason, Marin, and Logan, and the Ant chairs are by Arne Jacobsen.

STYLE GUIDE

■ Resist the urge to be too fancy. Sturdy furniture, hard-wearing surfaces, and fabrics that can be easily cleaned should be at the top of your list when it comes to decorating a room for a young child or teenager. Because this is your offspring's sanctuary, it should be one place they don't have to worry too much about stains, spills, and scratches.

■ Furnish your child's room in anticipation of sleepovers with friends. Bunk or trundle beds are obvious choices, but keeping an inflatable mattress on hand will do just fine.

■ Install a child-friendly sink in your youngster's bath; a long school-style vessel or one placed toddler height will make washing up more fun.

■ Nearly every young person goes through a poster phase. Survive it by installing a corkboard wall and providing a healthy supply of colorful pushpins.

■ Whether your child amasses odd rocks, china animals, or action figures, incorporate enough shelving to display his or her treasures. Lead by example: If you treat their pursuits seriously, hopefully they will respect and take interest in your more sophisticated collections too.

■ Most decorators we know swear they started out rearranging their family's furniture as children, so be open-minded: You might be giving a future Rose Tarlow her first commission.

LEFT
The Southampton, New York,
bedroom of Lily Krakoff, a daughter of Coach
president and executive creative
director Reed Krakoff and his interior decorator
wife, Delphine, features a daybed designed
by Delphine, a vintage Jean Royère
side chair, and a chest
hand-painted by artist Pierre Le-Tan.

OUTDOOR LIVING

TERRACES, GARDENS & POOLS

TERRACES, GARDENS & POOLS

Living life to the fullest means furnishing your outdoor spaces as mindfully as those indoors. Gardens, terraces, porches, verandas, and gazebos—these and other exterior areas open to fresh air and the beauty of nature offer rich decorative possibilities. So forget simply positioning a few teak chaise longues at the edge of a glittering pool and calling it a day. Think comfort, think drama, think elegance. A portico can be draped with flowing curtains of cotton duck, giving the appearance of a Grecian temple, while a generous veranda is a perfect site for deep-dish sofas, woven-raffia rugs, and white-painted tables arrayed with flickering hurricane lamps. Build an outdoor fireplace flanked by banquettes strewn with inviting cushions, or install an après-beach shower in the leafy embrace of a lush hedge of privet. Shade a stone terrace with grand panels of canvas stretched from the side of the house and attached to tall, sturdy poles ornamented with shining brass finials. A secluded porch outfitted as a satellite dining area is worth lingering on all afternoon, you and your guests seated in comfortable chairs gathered around a capacious table, cool mojitos in hand and a soft breeze rustling the trees. Potted plants, from lush Boston ferns to hibiscus standards, bring the garden even closer to home; or give wisteria or climbing jasmine—even grapevines—support by building an airy pergola. Whatever outdoor decor you settle on, maintenance will always be a critical part of the effect you're after. "Some people have an it-doesn't-matter-because-it's-only-outdoors attitude. The reason you are outdoors in the first place is to enjoy the cleanliness, the freshness," Billy Baldwin, dean of American decorating, wrote more than 30 years ago. "If you let the chairs rust and the cushions mildew, you destroy that pleasure." Happily, innovations in weather-resistant materials, especially fabrics and trimmings, have expanded the aesthetic options, inspiring homeowners to use their lawns and poolsides as stylish and colorful adjuncts for entertaining throughout the year. ■

PRECEDING PAGES
A table set for lunch on
the veranda of Porch House, decorator
Chessy Rayner's Southampton,
New York, home; the
glassware is Mexican, and the flowers
are from Rayner's garden.

OPPOSITE
The pool at the East Hampton,
New York, retreat
of designer Charlotte Moss and her husband,
Barry Friedberg, is surrounded
by a lush perennial garden, hedges of
boxwood, and a semicircular
bed of roses.

ABOVE
Shell-encrusted torchères crafted by
Andrew Fisher, a former protégé
of famed tastemaker Tony Duquette, stand guard
over the pool at the home Fisher
shares with decorator Jeffry Weisman in Sonoma County,
California; the teak chaises are a Weisman
design for the Wicker Works.

LEFT
A garden at the Millbrook, New York,
weekend house of jewelry designer
Mish Tworkowski and architect Joseph Singer
features a filigreed gazebo and
trelliswork fences
punctuated by ogee arches.

ABOVE
Part of an old barn at designer
Kathryn M. Ireland's farmhouse near Toulouse,
France, serves as a
rustic open-air dining room.

TOP RIGHT
Vegetable beds are bordered
with tidy boxwood at
landscape architect Arabella Lennox-Boyd's
estate, Gresgarth
Hall, in Lancashire, England.

CENTER RIGHT
Square-clipped chestnut
trees flank British decorator David Hicks's
Oxfordshire pool, which
gives onto an allée of untrimmed
chestnuts.

BOTTOM RIGHT
Baroque-style parterres
pattern the courtyard of Le Bâtiment,
conductor William Christie's
home near Thiré, France.

OPPOSITE
A lap pool reflects the
classical-inspired poolhouse designer
John Stedila built as a folly at his
Amagansett, New York,
weekend home.

ABOVE
In the living room of a
Dominican Republic getaway designed by architect
Hugh Newell Jacobsen for clients Georgia
and David Welles, louvered mahogany doors, painted white, open
completely to the pool terrace and a view of the sea,
yet close tight to shelter the
space from rain and tropical-storm winds.

RIGHT
The Welles house—crowned by a
wrought-iron sunburst weather vane—glows
at twilight.

OPPOSITE
Limned with rustic stone coping
and shaded by pine trees,
the swimming pool at Ricky and Ralph Lauren's
Montauk, New York, compound
resembles a secluded pond.

ABOVE
A columned pergola shelters the
Jeffrey Bilhuber–designed
poolhouse at the Bridgehampton, New York,
retreat of ad guru Trey Laird and
his wife, Jenny.

LEFT
Accessories designers
Richard Lambertson and John Truex
collaborated with
their friend Michael Trapp on the plan for
the garden at their Sharon,
Connecticut, country house.

ABOVE
Kelly Klein's iconic book *Pools* inspired
the photographer to design her own in Wellington,
Florida. Painted black and bordered in soapstone,
the pool features sculptural handrails.

TOP RIGHT
Philanthropists Frances and John Bowes
transplanted 125-year-old
olive trees from an abandoned grove not far from
their Sonoma Valley, California,
house to create a graceful
allée; the path is lined with rosemary.

CENTER RIGHT
Fashion designer Monique Lhuillier
and her husband, Tom Bugbee, erected a columned
pergola in their Bel Air, California, garden
and outfitted it with lean modern furniture.

BOTTOM RIGHT
Decorators Jeffry Weisman and Andrew Fisher
used a Sunbrella-fabric awning at their
hilltop home overlooking the Russian River Valley
in Northern California.

OPPOSITE
A terrace by the pool at Cindy Crawford
and Rande Gerber's Brentwood, California, house,
which was designed by Michael S. Smith,
includes a welcoming fireplace, a tile-top table and metal
chairs, and easygoing striped-canvas pillows.

"ONE WAY OR ANOTHER,
WATER HAS THE POWER TO EVOKE EMOTION
AND TRANSFORM US—AND ANYONE WHO GREW UP WITH A
POOL KNOWS HOW THOROUGHLY
IT CAN DEFINE THE WHOLE CHARACTER
OF SUMMER"

— *Martha Baker, landscape designer/author*

OPPOSITE
The tilework of the pool at interior designer
Juan Montoya's Hudson Valley, New York,
weekend house was inspired by a ballroom
floor at the Royal Palace in Stockholm.

ABOVE
Iranian architect Nasrine Faghih created a
dramatic indoor pool for the Provençal home
of an art-collector client; it is adjacent to an outdoor
pool and offers views of the French countryside.

STYLE GUIDE

▪ Flowers and shrubs aren't enough to make a garden, no matter how rare or beautiful the varieties. Benches and other types of practical seating will ensure that the plants you've cultivated can be admired by a solitary visitor or a group of friends. And choose styles and colors that will blend into the landscape rather than fight it.

▪ Make sure the seating in outdoor areas for entertaining is comfortable, and don't forget side and cocktail tables. Also take careful note of local climate conditions so you can select furniture whose materials will hold up to the elements; teak, fiberglass, and synthetic wicker are options that offer durability without compromising style.

▪ Provide shady retreats—such as under an awning, pergola, market umbrella, or spreading tree—so family and friends can gather for warm-weather meals and escape the sun's rays.

▪ Don't feel pressured to purchase an entire matching suite of outdoor furnishings. Choosing a mix of styles and materials allows you to express your personal taste just as you would in an indoor space.

▪ Once upon a time, shades of Caribbean blue were de rigueur for pools. Today, however, pools lined with dark colors such as gray or black give a natural look and also reflect the sky like a perfectly polished mirror.

▪ There is nothing more soothing than the sound of falling water—even a thin stream splashing into a small fountain will help create the luxurious feeling of an oasis and add a sense of calm to your garden.

RIGHT
At LongHouse, the East Hampton,
New York, retreat of
textile designer Jack Lenor Larsen,
16-foot columns topped with the runic symbol for
protection were installed at the edge
of a lotus pond; the Ming dynasty pots were once
used for transporting porcelain.

SOURCEBOOK

ACCESSORIES

Cartier
cartier.com

Dransfield & Ross
dransfieldandross.biz

Hable Construction
hableconstruction.com

Hermès
hermes.com

Kate Spade
katespade.com

Kenneth Wingard
kennethwingard.com

Larson-Juhl
larsonjuhl.com

Natural Curiosities
naturalcuriosities.com

Pearl River
pearlriver.com

Roberta Roller Rabbit
robertarollerrabbit.com

Ruzzetti and Gow
ruzzettiandgow.com

Smythson
smythson.com

Tiffany & Co.
tiffany.com

Verdura
verdura.com

Vivre
vivre.com

William Wayne & Co.
william-wayne.com

ART/ANTIQUES

1stdibs.com
1stdibs.com

Amy Perlin Antiques
amyperlinantiques.com

Artaissance
artthatfits.com

Artnet
artnet.com

Blackman Cruz
blackmancruz.com

Donzella 20th Century
Gallery
donzella.com

Duane
duanemodern.com

Galerie Van den Akker
*galerievandenakker-
.com*

JF Chen
jfchen.com

Todd Merrill Antiques
merrillantiques.com

BED/BATH LINENS

Ann Gish
anngish.com

Casa Del Bianco
casadelbianco.com

The Company
Store
thecompanystore.com

D. Porthault
dporthault.fr

DKNY Home
dknyhome.com

Dwell Studio
dwellstudio.com

Frette
frette.com

Garnet Hill
garnethill.com

John Robshaw
Textiles
johnrobshaw.com

Leontine Linens
leontinelinens.com

Matouk
matouk.com

Scandia Down
scandiadown.com

Sferra
sferralinens.com

EMPORIUM

ABC Carpet & Home
abchome.com

Aero
aerostudios.com

Ankasa
ankasa.com

Anthropologie
anthropologie.com

Apartment 48
apartment48.com

Armani/Casa
armanicasa.com

Arteriors Home
arteriorshome.com

Ballard Designs
ballarddesigns.com

Barneys New York
barneys.com

Belvedere
belvedereinc.com

Bergdorf Goodman
bergdorfgoodman.com

Bobo Intriguing Objects
bobointriguingobjects.com

Bottega Veneta
bottegaveneta.com

Calvin Klein Home
calvinklein.com

Casamidy
casamidy.com

CB2
cb2.com

Clearly First
clearlyfirst.com

The Conran Shop
conranusa.com

The Container
Store
thecontainerstore.com

Cost Plus World
Market
worldmarket.com

Crate & Barrel
crateandbarrel.com

Design Within
Reach
dwr.com

Flair
flairhomecollection.com

Gracious Home
gracioushome.com

Gump's
gumps.com

H. D. Buttercup
hdbuttercup.com

Hollyhock
hollyhockinc.com

Hollywood at
Home
hollywoodathome.com

IKEA
ikea.com

Intérieurs
interieurs.com

Jayson Home & Garden
*jaysonhomeandgarden-
.com*

John Derian
johnderian.com

Jonathan Adler
jonathanadler.com

Lars Bolander
larsbolander.com

Mecox Gardens
mecoxgardens.com

Moss
mossonline.com

Muji
muji.us

Neiman Marcus
neimanmarcus.com

Ochre
ochre.net

Oly
olystudio.com

Pierre Deux
pierredeux.com

Pottery Barn
potterybarn.com

Ralph Lauren
Home
ralphlaurenhome.com

Restoration Hardware
*restorationhardware-
.com*

Robb & Stucky
robbstucky.com

Room & Board
roomandboard.com

Suite New York
suiteny.com

Target
target.com

Todd Alexander
Romano
toddromanohome.com

Treillage
treillageonline.com

Vagabond Vintage
vagabondvintage.com

VW Home
vicentewolf.com

West Elm
westelm.com

Williams-Sonoma
Home
wshome.com

Wisteria
wisteria.com

FLOOR COVERINGS

Dash & Albert
dashandalbert.com

Elson & Co.
elsoncompany.com

Flor
flor.com

Madeline Weinrib Atelier
madelineweinrib.com

Mansour Modern
mansourmodern.com

Odegard
odegardinc.com

The Rug
Company
therugcompany.info

Safavieh
safavieh.com

Tufenkian Artisan
Carpets
tufenkian.com

FURNITURE
American Leather
americanleather-.com

B&B Italia
bebitalia.it

Baker
bakerfurniture.com

BDDW
bddw.com

Bernhardt
bernhardt.com

BoConcept
boconcept.com

Calligaris
calligaris.it

Cassina USA
cassinausa.com

Century Furniture
www.centuryfurni-ture.com

DDC
ddcnyc.com

Elite Leather
eliteleather.com

George Smith
georgesmith.com

Hickory Chair
hickorychair.com

Janus et Cie
janusetcie.com

Julian Chichester
julianchichester.com

Knoll
knoll.com

Lee Industries
leeindustries.com

Ligne Roset
ligne-roset-usa.com

McGuire
mcguirefurniture.com

Mitchell Gold +
Bob Williams
mgandbw.com

Montauk Sofa
montauksofa.com

Natuzzi
natuzzi.com

Roche Bobois
rochebobois.com

Stickley
stickley.com

Thomasville
thomasville.com

Wunderley
wunderley.com

KITCHEN/BATH
Boffi
boffi.com

Bosch
boschappliances.com

Bulthaup
bulthaup.com

Dornbracht USA
dornbracht.com

Duravit
duravit.com

Electrolux
electroluxusa.com

Elkay
elkayusa.com

GE
geappliances.com

Jenn-Air
jennair.com

Kallista
kallista.com

Kitchen Aid
kitchenaid.com

Kohler
kohler.com

LG Electronics
lgusa.com

Miele
miele.com

Robern
robern.com

Rohl
rohlhome.com

Sub-Zero
subzero.com

Thermador
thermador.com

Urban Archaeology
urbanarchaeology.com

Viking
vikingrange.com

Vitraform
vitraform.com

Waterworks
waterworks.com

Wolf
wolfappliance.com

LIGHTING
Artemide
artemide.us

Christopher Spitzmiller
christopherspitzmiller-.com

Circa Lighting
circalighting.com

Flos
flos.com

Schoolhouse Electric
schoolhouseelectric.com

Visual Comfort & Co.
visualcomfort.com

PAINT
Benjamin Moore
benjaminmoore.com

Donald Kaufman Color
donaldkaufmancolor-.com

Farrow & Ball
farrow-ball.com

Mythic Paint
mythicpaint.com

Pratt & Lambert
Paints
prattandlambert.com

Sherwin-Williams
sherwin-williams.com

TABLETOP
Baccarat
baccarat.com

Christofle
christofle.com

Elements
elementschicago-.com

Gearys
gearys.com

Haviland
haviland-limoges-.com

Juliska
juliska.com

Kiln Design
Studio
kilnenamel.com

Match
match1995.com

Michael Aram
michaelaram.com

Michael C. Fina
michaelcfina.com

Moser
www.moserusa.com

Mottahedeh
mottahedeh.com

Reed & Barton
reedandbarton.com

Steuben Glass
steuben.com

Sur La Table
surlatable.com

Vietri
vietri.com

Waterford
waterford.com

Wedgwood
wedgwood.com

William Yeoward Crystal
williamyeowardcrystal-.com

TEXTILES/WALL COVERINGS
Iksel Decorative Arts
iksel.com

Les Indiennes
lesindiennes.com

The Silk Trading Co.
silktrading.com

Sunbrella
sunbrella.com

TILE/SURFACES
Ann Sacks
annsacks.com

Artistic Tile
artistictile.com

Bisazza
bisazza.com

Compas
compasstone.com

DuPont Corian
corian.com

Exquisite Surfaces
xsurfaces.com

Sicis
sicis.com

PHOTO CREDITS

Page 125: Simon Upton *(Dec 06)*

Page 126: Henry Bourne *(Oct 03)*

Page 127: Roger Davies, top *(Apr 09)*; Pieter Estersohn, bottom *(Oct 04)*

Page 128: William Waldron *(Sept 08)*

Page 129: Gilles de Chabaneix, top *(Feb 91)*; Simon Upton, bottom *(Mar 09)*

Page 130: Eric Piasecki, top *(Sept 07)*; Andrew Garn, bottom *(Feb/Mar 92)*

Page 131: Grey Crawford *(Jul/Aug 05)*

Page 132: Pieter Estersohn *(Apr 03)*

Page 133: William Waldron *(Jan/Feb 09)*

Page 134: Guillaume de Laubier, top *(Apr/May 94)*; Tim Street-Porter, bottom *(Aug 90)*

Page 135: Henry Bourne *(Aug/Sept 97)*

Pages 136–37: William Abranowicz *(Dec/Jan 92)*

Page 141: Pieter Estersohn *(Dec/Jan 95)*

Page 142: Laura Resen *(Nov 01)*

Page 143: William Waldron, top *(Dec 05)*; Laura Resen, bottom *(Aug/Sept 03)*

Page 144: John M. Hall *(Dec/Jan 95)*

Page 145: Simon Upton, top *(Mar 06)*; William Waldron, bottom *(Oct 04)*

Page 146: Fernando Bengoechea, top *(May 98)*; William Waldron, bottom *(May 07)*

Page 147: Simon Upton *(Dec 05)*

Pages 148–49: Fernando Bengoechea *(Apr/May 97)*

Page 150: Simon Upton *(Apr 06)*

Page 151: William Abranowicz *(Nov 02)*

Page 152: Pieter Estersohn *(Apr 05)*

Page 153: William Waldron, top *(Sept 05)*; Jacques Dirand, bottom *(Dec/Jan 92)*

Page 154: François Dischinger *(Mar 05)*

Page 155: Pieter Estersohn, top *(Apr 02)* and bottom *(Apr/May 96)*

Page 156: Pieter Estersohn, top left *(Jan/Feb 06)*; Henry Bourne, top right *(May 04)*; Simon Upton, bottom *(Aug/Sept 03)*; John M. Hall, center left *(Jun/Jul 92)*

Page 157: Fernando Bengoechea *(May 01)*

Page 158: William Waldron *(Jan/Feb 09)*

Page 159: Henry Bourne, top *(Nov 98)*; Jacques Dirand, bottom *(Jun/Jul 98)*

Page 160: William Waldron *(Nov 01)*

Page 161: Simon Upton *(Sept 06)*

Page 162: Simon Upton, top *(Sept 06)*; Thibault Jeanson, bottom *(Dec/Jan 96)*

Page 163: Fernando Bengoechea *(Oct 05)*

Page 164: Vicente Wolf *(May 02)*

Page 165: Simon Upton, top *(Apr 07)*;

Joshua McHugh, bottom *(May 04)*

Page 166: Simon Upton, top *(Oct 06)*; Henry Bourne, bottom *(Mar 07)*

Page 167: Pieter Estersohn *(Dec/Jan 03)*

Page 168: Henry Bourne *(Feb/Mar 02)*

Page 169: Peter Woloszynski, top *(Dec/Jan 95)*; Simon Upton, bottom *(Nov 06)*

Page 170: William Waldron, top *(May 04)* and bottom *(May 07)*

Page 171: Pieter Estersohn *(Jun/Jul 03)*

Page 172: William Waldron *(Jun/Jul 02)*

Page 173: Paul Warchol *(Apr 90)*

Pages 174–75: Simon Upton *(Nov 06)*

Page 176: Grey Crawford *(Nov 04)*

Page 177: Henry Bourne, left *(Feb/Mar 01)*; William Waldron, top right *(Jun/Jul 04)*; Simon Upton, bottom *(Nov 07)*

Page 178: Simon Upton, top left *(Mar 07)*; Jen Fong, top right *(Oct/Nov 96)*; Timothy White, center right *(Jun/Jul 93)*; Joshua McHugh, bottom *(May 08)*

Page 179: Pieter Estersohn *(Feb/Mar 04)*

Page 180: William Waldron *(Sept 08)*

Page 181: Simon Upton, top *(Oct 06)*; Marianne Haas, center *(Apr 00)*; Eric Boman, bottom *(Sept 09)*

Page 182: Henry Bourne *(Feb/Mar 99)*

Page 184: Robert Lautman, top *(Feb 91)*; Henry Bourne, bottom *(Apr 04)*

Page 185: Simon Upton *(Jan/Feb 09)*

Page 186: Pieter Estersohn *(Apr 03)*

Page 187: William Waldron *(Jan/Feb 06)*

Page 188: Fernando Bengoechea, top left *(Aug/Sept 00)*; Pieter Estersohn, right *(Aug/Sept 96)* and bottom left *(Aug/Sept 98)*

Page 189: Roger Davies *(Dec 08)*

Page 190: William Waldron *(May 07)*

Page 191: Pieter Estersohn, top *(Jun/Jul 03)*; Minh + Wass, bottom *(Jun/Jul 97)*

Page 192: Vicente Wolf *(May 02)*

Page 193: Vicente Wolf, top *(May 02)*; Joshua McHugh, bottom *(Nov 08)*

Page 194: William Waldron, top *(May 08)*; Dominique Vorillon, bottom right *(Jun/Jul 03)*; Marianne Haas, bottom left *(Dec/Jan 97)*; Henry Bourne, center left *(Aug/Sept 95)*

Page 195: Fernando Bengoechea *(Oct 00)*

Page 196: Simon Upton *(Oct 07)*

Page 197: Eric Piasecki, top *(Jul/Aug 08)*; Henry Bourne, bottom *(Dec/Jan 01)*

Page 198: Roger Davies *(Jan/Feb 08)*

Page 199: Grey Crawford *(Jul/Aug 05)*

Page 200: Marianne Haas *(Aug 90)*

Page 201: Pieter Estersohn, top *(Jan/Feb 06)*; Henry Bourne, bottom *(Apr 04)*

Page 202: Henry Bourne *(Jun/Jul 95)*

Page 203: John M. Hall *(Jun/Jul 90)*

Page 204: William Waldron, top left *(Jun/Jul 04)*; Simon Upton, top right *(Feb/Mar 04)*; Jacques Dirand, bottom *(Jun/Jul 98)*; Pieter Estersohn, center left *(Aug/Sept 98)*

Page 205: Jacques Dirand *(Jun/Jul 98)*

Pages 206–07: Laura Resen *(Aug/Sept 04)*

Page 208: Grey Crawford *(Jun 05)*

Page 210: Pieter Estersohn, top *(Nov 05)*; Eric Piasecki, bottom right *(Sept 06)*; Dominique Vorillon, bottom left *(Jun/Jul 03)*

Page 211: Pieter Estersohn *(Feb/Mar 03)*

Page 212: Timothy Kolk, top left *(Jul/Aug 07)*; William Waldron, top right *(Jun/Jul 04)*; Simon Upton, bottom *(Oct 06)*

Page 213: William Abranowicz *(Nov 00)*

Page 214: William Waldron *(Sept 08)*

Page 215: Pieter Estersohn, top left *(Jan/Feb 06)*; William Waldron, top right *(Jul/Aug 08)*; Simon Upton, center right *(Jan/Feb 09)*; William Waldron, bottom *(Nov 06)*

Pages 216–17: Reed Krakoff *(Sept 06)*

Page 221: Karen Radkai *(Sept 90)*

Page 222: Pieter Estersohn *(Apr 02)*

Page 223: Grey Crawford, top *(Feb/Mar 03)*; William Waldron, bottom *(May 08)*

Page 224: Henry Bourne, top left *(Feb/Mar 02)*; Jerry Harpur, top right *(Apr/May 94)*; Dana Hyde, center right *(Aug 91)*; Gary Gunderson, bottom *(Jun 07)*

Page 225: Simon Upton *(Jun/Jul 02)*

Page 226: Robert Lautman *(Winter 90)*

Page 227: Robert Lautman *(Winter 90)*

Page 228: Pieter Estersohn *(Jul/Aug 05)*

Page 229: Pieter Estersohn, top *(Jul/Aug 07)* and bottom *(Oct 08)*

Page 230: William Waldron, top left *(May 07)*; Marion Brenner, top right *(Feb/Mar 00)*; Roger Davies, center right *(Jan/Feb 08)*; Grey Crawford, bottom *(Sept 08)*

Page 231: Pieter Estersohn *(Oct 02)*

Page 232: Pieter Estersohn *(Jun/Jul 04)*

Page 233: Jean-Pierre Godeaut *(Jun/Jul 91)*

Pages 234–35: Todd Eberle *(Sept 91)*

Back cover: Simon Upton *(Apr 06)*

ACKNOWLEDGMENTS

Style and Substance: The Best of ELLE DECOR salutes the vision of ELLE DECOR's founding international director Jean Demachy and publication director Régis Pagniez; Jean launched French ELLE DÉCORATION and inspired all subsequent editions, and Régis guided our own formative years with his exacting eye. The talents of editors Barbara L. Dixon (1989–90), Louis Oliver Gropp (1990–91), and Marian McEvoy (1991–2000) are clearly reflected in this book as well; each contributed enormously to ELLE DECOR's early growth and success, as did Charles C. Bricker Jr., Elizabeth Sverbeyeff Byron, and Regina Clarbour.

This book would not have been possible without the generous and consistent support of several people, including Alain Lemarchand, Philippe Guelton, Deborah Burns, Barbara Friedmann, Ronald Minutella, and Jack Kliger. And I am deeply grateful for the advice, wisdom, and friendship that Jean-Louis Ginibre, my mentor and former editorial director, has so kindly shared over the past 20 years.

I thank Dorothée Walliser, head of Filipacchi Publishing, for spearheading this project, Lynn Scaglione for managing its completion with remarkable patience and ease, and Annie Andres for overseeing our color reproduction.

I'm truly indebted to our extraordinary ELLE DECOR team—in particular, design and decoration editor Anita Sarsidi and editor at large Mitchell Owens, who have been key members of the magazine's family on and off for two decades. Their brilliant work is showcased in ELLE DECOR month after month and is an essential part of this book.

The elegant mind-set of art director Florentino Pamintuan is evident on every page of *Style and Substance,* and he deftly made even the archival photos look fresh and new; layouts were refined with thoughtful precision by designer Katherine McDonald; copy chief Kate Hambrecht edited with meticulous care; and assistant editor Lindsey Nelson painstakingly researched and checked the text. Our photo editor Tara Germinsky called in images from around the world that had appeared in 156 issues of ELLE DECOR—a nearly unimaginable feat. And the consummate focus and dedication of assistant managing editor Dara Keithley deserves special recognition.

The designers, architects, and tastemakers who created the rooms featured on these pages, however, are our true stars; they inform and inspire us—and ELLE DECOR's readers—every day. I thank the editors and stylists who produced the selected photographs—especially our own style-setter, editor at large Carlos Mota—and the writers whose work is not utilized in *Style and Substance* but whom we hold in such high esteem. I owe deepest gratitude to the photographers who documented two decades of interiors—and the lives behind them—for us. The images by photographers Fernando Bengoechea, Henry Bourne, Grey Crawford, Roger Davies, Jacques Dirand, Pieter Estersohn, Marianne Haas, John M. Hall, Thibault Jeanson, Joshua McHugh, Simon Upton, Dominique Vorillon, and William Waldron, among others, are simply sublime. And the creativity, artful intelligence, joie de vivre, and grace that our dear friend Fernando Bengoechea brought to us at ELLE DECOR are never far from my thoughts; it is to his memory that I dedicate this book.

MARGARET RUSSELL
SUMMER 2009